THE
YOU
YOU NEVER
KNEW

THE
YOU
YOU NEVER
KNEW

Rewire Your Body and Mind
to Go from Trauma and Stress
to Health and Happiness

NATE ORTIZ

BenBella

BenBella Books, Inc.
Dallas, TX

BenBella

BenBella Books, Inc.
8080 N. Central Expressway
Suite 1700
Dallas, TX 75206
benbellabooks.com
Send feedback to feedback@benbellabooks.com

BenBella is a federally registered trademark.

Printed in the United States of America
10 9 8 7 6 5 4 3 2 1

Library of Congress Control Number: 2024039022
ISBN 9781637745472 (trade paperback)
ISBN 9781637745489 (electronic)

Editing by Leah Wilson
Copyediting by Elizabeth Degenhard
Proofreading by Ashley Casteel and Cape Cod Compositors, Inc.
Indexing by WordCo Indexing Services
Text design and composition by Aaron Edmiston
Cover design by Brigid Pearson
Cover image © Adobe Stock / Eigens
Printed by Lake Book Manufacturing

This book is dedicated to my father,
my mother, and my brothers.

And to Haskiri, my biggest supporter and love.

CONTENTS

CONTENTS

YOU ARE NOT BROKEN

Let me guess: you've tried everything to improve your health and sense of well-being. You've consulted therapists, bought weight-loss programs, and have five different probiotics in your cabinet. But no matter how much yoga you do or meditation you try, your body still aches and your mind is unsettled. You are reading this book now because you want solutions to your problems and relief from suffering.

What if I said that you could eliminate most of your mental, physical, and emotional frustrations by reading this book and applying its core principles? You could have more control over your thoughts, improve physical movement, and manage your emotions in any situation. You could consistently achieve your goals, feel less bloated, and maintain healthier relationships. I am telling you: this is attainable. Believe it or not, you already have everything you need to make those changes. Put this system to work, and you will accomplish all of the above. Forget all your preexisting beliefs about health and wellness. Are you ready to fully heal?

I know this might feel like it's impossible for you. You might feel like something's broken inside you, a sensation I've known all too well. It's a feeling that often emerges in the wake of trauma, ushering in a host of challenges that extend beyond mental health—a reality I've navigated throughout my life.

A HISTORY OF TRAUMA

I came into this world traumatized. Born with drugs in my system, I was immediately rushed to the intensive care unit, missing out on having my first experience in this world be in the arms of my mother. In the ICU, I fought for my life from withdrawal, which gave me seizures. The battle was tough, and there were times the doctors didn't think I would make it.

At the hospital, my family was told I would have issues for the rest of my life and might need a personal care assistant. My father never believed that. He was confident he could take care of me himself and I would be just fine. I've always believed that fight for survival, and my father's faith in me, subconsciously prepared me for the years of trauma to come.

After a long struggle in the ICU, it was time for me to go home. I've heard many stories about what happened that day, but I will tell you the story that has been most consistent. Neither of my parents picked me up. My grandmother from my mother's side did. My mother, Marybeth, still had her soon-to-be-ex-husband's last name, Ortiz, and since my father, Nathan Turner, wasn't there to sign my birth certificate, I didn't get his last name, Turner. Instead, they named me Nathan Ortiz. What a way to start life, huh?

I am biracial, with a Black father and a white mother. This made me brown—not Black enough to be Black nor white enough to be white—and created many identity problems for me. The fact that my last name was Ortiz made things even more confusing.

Growing up, my life was far from stable. Just a few years after I was born, my mom went to prison, leaving me without a real home. I was shuffled between my dad, who was living with his own mother, and my maternal grandmother. Moving from one family member's house to another deepened the uncertainty in my heart, leaving me always wondering where I truly belonged.

My dad was a great father. He was also a drug dealer who did what he felt necessary to provide for us. I can still vividly remember the secretive exchanges of small white bags for tightly rubber-banded cash. This aspect of my father's life was something I became aware of early, at age four, during two terrifying robbery attempts. The first time, a gunman pointed his weapon directly at me while demanding money from my dad. The second was even more terrifying, with my dad pushing me in a stroller, racing away as bullets whizzed past us. These incidents left deep scars. From that moment on, sudden noises like a car horn would make me jump, and the sight of any man approaching filled me with a dread so intense I would brace myself, fearing it might be another robbery.

These moments of terror taught me to always be on guard and marked the beginning of a lifelong struggle with anxiety and trust issues, particularly with strangers. I never allowed myself to fully fall asleep, fearing someone might come to hurt me when I was at my most vulnerable and unaware. Emotionally, I was wary even of those who tried to help me, including teachers, family members, and friends. As much as I wanted to believe in their kindness, I couldn't shake the fear that it was just a precursor to harm. For these reasons, I never asked for help, choosing to rely solely on my own judgment. I raised myself, along with my two younger brothers, and grew up fast. I didn't have a childhood. I was a parent and an adult at a young age.

I was relieved when my mom got out of prison and regained custody of my siblings and me. At eight years old, I was thrilled to finally have a place that felt like a home. However, that joy was short-lived. Almost immediately, my mother became abusive, resorting to bats, belts, and even a knife—which I narrowly escaped thanks to an unlocked door. Her new boyfriend was just as violent. Access to food was unreliable as well. On the days our food stamp benefits arrived, my mother would trade them for drugs and get high. Locked out of our apartment, my siblings and I often slept in the hallway, hungry. My older brother, driven to desperation, began stealing from supermarkets to feed us.

Ashamed and scared, I hid the truth about what was happening at home from my teachers and school counselors. Despite the pain I was enduring, I was terrified of the consequences of speaking out. I feared that telling someone risked my mother returning to prison and my brothers and me returning to the instability of moving from house to house. So, I kept silent, carrying the burden alone in hopes of keeping what little stability we had.

I often felt like I was a problem to other people. I stuttered as a child, and some family members and teachers were frustrated whenever I tried communicating with them. My older siblings distanced themselves from me, claiming I wasn't their real brother because we had different fathers. While their father was Puerto Rican, mine was Black. Being mixed white and Puerto Rican was common in the Holland Gardens projects where I grew up in Jersey City, New Jersey. Many of my cousins and friends were of mixed white and Puerto Rican heritage. I was the first one in my family with a Black father, and my siblings never let me forget that.

We played some fun games in the projects, such as manhunt, house, and rollerblading. I always looked forward to playing with my siblings, cousins, and their friends, but they didn't feel the same. They found ways to keep me from participating, and I'd be left alone, sad and hurt. I would cry, watching them play, but cheering from the sideline. They teased me and called me a big crybaby and said that was why they didn't play with me.

I missed sleepover parties because I was a bed wetter. I also struggled to control my bowel movements and sometimes pooped myself. Because of this, my family started calling me "Dookie," a slang term for poop. Over time, this nickname got shortened to "Dunna," but it remained an embarrassing reminder.

As I got older, I couldn't help but feel like I was broken. I was diagnosed with ADHD, dyslexia, and three autoimmune diseases, not to mention the mental weight of anxiety and depression. I asked the doctors, "Why do I have so many health problems?" They responded with one word, "Genetics," and then wrote me another prescription.

I became frustrated with my mind and body, but instead of giving up, I took action. I dedicated my life to studying the science behind my trauma and the connections between that trauma and my mental and physical health. This journey not only proved to me that I wasn't broken, but also set me on a path of self-discovery and acceptance. Shifting from self-judgment to self-understanding, I began to heal.

That's a journey I want for you, too. Maybe your story looks a little, or a lot, like mine. Maybe it doesn't. I've been holistically coaching clients for nearly a decade, and during that time I've coached wealthy celebrities and I've coached people living in poverty. Regardless of their background, every client came to me with the same underlying issue: they felt "stuck" when trying to transform into a happier, healthier version of themselves. They wrestled with unhealthy eating and exercise habits, felt guilty when setting boundaries by saying "no" to family and friends, and struggled to take the necessary actions for change despite knowing what to do, which led them to feel unfixable, born with bad luck, or, as many clients described it—*broken*. If past trauma has left you suffering from chronic health issues, if you feel anxious and stuck, this book is for you.

MISUNDERSTOOD— NOT BROKEN

I remember, at twenty-two, pouring my last dollar into a laptop and camera, fueled by the dream of launching my career and sharing insights on healing from trauma and stress. When I first tried to use the camera, however, it just wouldn't focus. Convinced it was the lens, I exchanged my last bit of money for a new one, yet faced the same issue. My frustration peaked as I stormed back to the store, convinced they'd sold me a faulty product.

The store clerk, with a calm demeanor, took the camera and pressed a few buttons. It focused perfectly. "Ah, you didn't adjust the settings," he noted.

"Settings?" I shot back, clearly annoyed.

He smiled. "This camera is among the best, quite special, but it requires understanding its settings to truly shine."

My frustration stemmed from a false perception, born out of not understanding the potential of what I had in my hands. My camera wasn't broken. I just didn't understand how to adjust the settings. Once I did, I was able to fully harness the camera's potential. Our bodies are the same. It isn't until we understand how trauma affects our internal settings that we are finally able to start healing. Trauma creates imbalances in our minds, bodies, and emotions that make us believe we are broken. The solution isn't a new lens or a different camera. It's understanding how to use what we already possess. Our journey through trauma and stress is about learning to adjust our internal settings—our attitudes, our beliefs, and, particularly, our nervous system.

Your nervous system is designed to respond and adjust to life's daily stressors. It's a complex network that senses our surroundings, influences our reactions, and shapes our emotions.

Under typical conditions, the nervous system helps us navigate stress. It allocates resources like our attention and energy to where they're needed most. It then returns to a state of balance after the stressor has passed. Returning to equilibrium is crucial for maintaining mental and physical health.

However, when faced with traumatic events, this finely tuned system can become disrupted. Our neural pathways are rewired to anticipate danger, creating what mental health professionals call a *sensitive nervous system*. An untraumatized nervous system returns to equilibrium after a stressful event. In contrast, a sensitive nervous system stays on high alert, turning even minor stressors into strong winds that threaten to knock us off balance.

Let's consider a real-world example: imagine two people, Quinn and Jamie, stuck in traffic. For Quinn, who has a well-regulated nervous system, the situation is annoying but manageable. He takes a deep breath, listens to some music, and uses the time to mentally prepare for the day ahead. His nervous system acknowledges the stressor and initiates a mild stress response to keep him alert but largely remains in balance, which allows Quinn to remain calm and focused.

For Jamie, who has a sensitive nervous system, the same traffic jam triggers a cascade of stress reactions. Her heart rate accelerates, her palms sweat, and her mind races with worries about being late and throwing off the day's schedule. This intense reaction isn't just about the traffic—it's the result of a nervous system that amplifies the stressor and also makes it harder to return to a state of calm.

Jamie's body responds chemically as if confronting a severe threat. This results in feelings of anxiety disproportionate to the actual scenario. It's not merely the external stressor that creates the problem; it's the internal reaction of an overreactive nervous system that amplifies the situation, complicating the search for peace and balance.

LIFE WITH A SENSITIVE NERVOUS SYSTEM

Navigating life with a sensitive nervous system is like maintaining balance on a tightrope. It is an act of focus, every single day, to not be overwhelmed by the stress that life throws at you. Common stressors—sudden loud noises, a fast-paced lifestyle, lack of sleep, worries about financial stability—can easily throw you off.

Early in life, this balancing act is often hidden behind the energy of youth. Despite difficult home lives or internal struggles, we manage to keep moving forward. We propel ourselves through school, work, and the pursuit of our ambitions by sheer force of will and the drive to survive.

However, this changes as we transition into adulthood. The adrenaline that once fueled us starts to fade, and the weight of adult responsibilities becomes more tangible. Now, without the daily structure of school and the support of teachers, counselors, and coaches, we face the realities of adult life—paying rent, securing employment, and managing finances. Often, we do so without guidance, as our families and communities may still be struggling themselves, lacking the resources or stability to provide the support we need.

As these pressures build, they start to affect us physically, mentally, and emotionally. Physically, we might notice an increase in weight that doesn't shed as easily as before, along with chronic muscle pain and digestive issues. Mentally, the challenges intensify; staying positive becomes harder as we struggle with procrastination, overthinking, and perfectionism. These changes contribute to an overwhelming emotional load, making it increasingly difficult for us to stay grounded and calm. And it can feel like nothing we try to fix our mental and physical issues is making a dent.

Believe me, I've been there. But everything changed when I realized that my health problems were deeply tied to my past traumas, and that by learning to manage my sensitive nervous system, I gained the power to rewire my mind, body, and emotions. You too can harness this power to heal and thrive.

Once I saw the difference managing my sensitive nervous system made in my health and quality of life, I couldn't keep this knowledge to myself—I had to share it with others who were suffering the way I had. So, I started spreading the word through every channel available to me.

As I shared my journey and strategies online, I was amazed to see my message resonate with millions. Now, I run workshops, offer one-on-one coaching, foster an engaged online community, and use my social media platforms to extend my reach. Through these avenues, I've been able to guide thousands of individuals from a state of trauma and stress to one of health and happiness.

In my eight years of coaching, I've seen my own struggles with a sensitive nervous system mirrored in the lives of countless clients. They come to me with a range of issues, which often include:

- Trauma and stress responses that show up as anxiety, frustration, and being overwhelmed
- Fatigue (usually low energy in the morning and an energy dip in the afternoon)
- Digestive issues
- Weight problems (can't lose weight or put on muscle)

- Inflammation, such as bloating, inflamed pelvic floor, or joint and muscle pain
- Hip, back, and neck pain (often arising from posture problems, such as muscular imbalances and misalignments in the spine)
- Hormonal imbalances
- Sleep issues
- No connection to purpose
- No support system and issues with their family and friends
- Struggles with doubt, confusion, or overthinking
- Being stuck in survival mode

I've also seen how traditional health and fitness programs *just don't work* for people with sensitive nervous systems. Guidelines from health experts, articles, and influencers who hadn't experienced trauma or didn't keep those with trauma in mind were ineffective. Frustrated clients got no results because their nervous systems were already on edge, stuck in a fight, flight, or freeze mode that left them too exhausted to maintain consistency in their health routines or daily responsibilities. These clients usually gained weight and became more bloated when following these programs. And they felt like *they* were the problem—that they were doing something wrong or not trying as hard as other people.

Most people come into the healing process ready to make a genuine, earnest effort. They're open, trusting, and ready to make a change. They diligently follow guidance and fully invest in trying to transform themselves. Yet, because they are missing that critical piece of understanding, that their challenges are stemming from their own body's unique responses to stress and trauma, they don't get the results they're looking for.

When the strategies they've been given fail to provide relief, it's not just physical pain that intensifies—so does emotional and mental distress. The disappointment of not finding success with conventional advice compounds their frustration, and now they are not only battling the original issues, but also dealing with the additional stress of feeling lost in their healing journey.

In their search for relief, clients often find themselves consulting with a wide array of health practitioners. This can range from traditional medical and therapeutic support, such as chiropractors, therapists, and medical doctors, to more holistic and alternative care providers, including personal trainers, nutritionists, massage therapists, Reiki coaches, and naturopathic doctors. When I coach someone, my goal is to save them as much money and time as possible while educating them on managing their mind, body, and emotions and helping them change their perception of themselves. And now, with this book, I can do the same for you.

By embracing the insights and strategies in this book, you're set to experience a profound shift. You'll notice changes in your emotional responses, thought patterns, and actions, leading you to uncover and embrace an aspect of your identity that has remained hidden beneath layers of past experiences and stress: a resilient, capable self that has always been part of you, waiting to be revealed. This is *The You You Never Knew*—the version of you that's not defined by trauma but by strength and potential.

You are not broken. You hold the power to redefine your well-being. We'll start this transformative journey by learning more about your sensitive nervous system in the next chapter.

2

THE FIVE LAYERS OF ENERGY

Trauma isn't something that is easily forgotten or over-looked. It doesn't just show up and then leave. And it isn't just a matter of mindset. Research in psychology has shown that trauma is retained in the body through the changes it drives in our biological stress response.[1]

Imagine someone who experienced trauma in their childhood home. Years later, merely walking down the street of their old neighborhood or standing in front of their old house can trigger overwhelming feelings. It's not just a flood of memories; it's as if they're transported back in time, experiencing the emotions and possibly even the physical sensations of those early years. Their body's reaction mirrors how it responded to the stressful or traumatic events back then—heart racing, palms sweating, an urge to flee.

This vivid re-experiencing illustrates how deeply the nervous system holds onto past traumas and how strongly it reacts to environments or situations that mirror those original moments of distress. It highlights the lasting impact of childhood trauma and how certain triggers, even decades later, can evoke a response as if the trauma was happening all over again.

Why does this happen? Research has demonstrated that individuals with post-traumatic stress disorder (PTSD) stemming from childhood trauma and abuse have average resting cortisol levels up to 60 percent higher than normal. Cortisol is a hormone produced by the adrenal glands that helps regulate stress responses, metabolism, and immune function. Furthermore, cortisol levels can soar to 122 percent higher than average when a new stressor is introduced—even when that stressor is unrelated to their past trauma.[2] Evidence suggests that a history of physical intimate partner violence also correlates with higher cortisol levels, particularly in women, compared to individuals who have not experienced such abuse.[3]

Trauma's ongoing effect on cortisol levels is important because cortisol, in partnership with adrenaline (another critical hormone in the body's response to stress), activates the sympathetic nervous system. Typically, this system is activated only when immediate threats are detected, priming the body for the *fight-or-flight* response. However, in individuals with trauma, cortisol levels are always elevated—meaning that their sympathetic nervous system can be on high alert even at rest. As a result, when a stressor does occur, this already primed system reacts more quickly and intensely than it normally would, as we saw with Jamie in the last chapter.

This overreaction can disrupt normal physiological functions. As the body diverts energy to more critical survival functions, digestion is frequently shut down. Stored sugars are quickly released to provide immediate energy, which spikes blood sugar levels, and heart rate increases to pump more blood to vital organs and muscles. These responses, while beneficial in actual dangerous situations, can become problematic when triggered too frequently or intensely.

This constant state of alert not only wears out physical systems but also leads to significant mental and emotional strain. Many of us experience heightened anxiety, mental fatigue, and emotional sensitivity to seemingly minor stressors, both real and perceived.

So, as you can see, trauma impacts more than just our minds. It fundamentally rewires our mind, body, and emotions, affecting us daily, often without our awareness. For me, learning how trauma affects our body and daily life long after the traumatic events have occurred was an eye-opening experience. It became clear that healing from trauma requires a holistic approach, one that considers the entire person. And that healing begins with understanding the *five layers of energy*.

REWIRED

Think of your body as being made up of five "layers of energy": the nervous system, organs and glands, muscular system, emotions, and subconscious mind. Each of these layers represents a source of strength and vitality, essential for sustained physical and mental activity. These layers are also interconnected; the vitality of each layer directly influences and strengthens the next. When these layers are in balance, the layers support one another, creating a dynamic interplay that impacts your overall well-being. But living with a sensitive nervous system throws all of these layers off balance.

It begins with the first layer of energy, your *nervous system*. The nervous system is activated whenever your senses (sight, sound, smell, taste, and touch) perceive a threat. When your nervous system is sensitive, it responds more quickly and intensely to stimuli. Certain senses can also trigger memories from past traumatic events, leading you to react as if that traumatic event is happening in the moment.

For example, the sound of loud noises, like a car horn, used to trigger a subconscious reaction from me because my brain associated loud noises with the gunshots from the robberies I survived as a child. And when someone walked toward me with aggression or resembled the robbers in any way, my senses immediately kicked into high gear, preparing me for a potential threat—triggering the fight-or-flight response as a means of ensuring my safety.

These overreactions to sensory stimuli activate the second energy layer—*organs and glands*. The hypothalamus, pituitary, and adrenal glands oversee the body's hormonal responses, such as the release of adrenaline and cortisol. These glands and the stress hormones they release fire up the body's fight-or-flight response, increasing the heart rate to supply more blood and redirecting that blood flow from organs such as the stomach and intestines to the brain, heart, lungs, and muscles—parts of the body needed for physical action. This reduces digestive activity and expands the lungs to take in more oxygen.

The collaborative effort of the nervous system and the organs and glands readies your *muscular system*—the third layer. This interconnected network of nerves and muscles controls your physical reactions. In response to elevated stress hormones, as part of your natural defense mechanisms, your muscles tense up in preparation to confront a potential threat.

Once the body is primed for action, it heightens the fourth layer of energy, your *emotions*. As your organs and muscles experience physiological changes—the heart starts racing, the lungs work harder to pump out more air, and the muscles brace themselves for fight or flight—these physical sensations then give rise to *feelings*, as your brain interprets and gives meaning to what you are experiencing physically. The body's physical overreaction to stimuli also leads to an emotional overreaction, making us seem overly anxious or upset.

From these feelings arise thoughts, your brain's attempt to make sense of what you're feeling. It's here that you construct mental narratives around your experiences, in an attempt to understand and be able to predict your environment—a necessary step to keep yourself safe. These thoughts lay the groundwork for the fifth layer, your *subconscious mind*.

The subconscious mind is the storage space for past experiences, memories, and learned behaviors. It profoundly influences how you view the world and interact with your environment, frequently driving your actions and decisions without your full awareness. There are two ways things enter your subconscious mind. The first is through repetition. The second is through trauma.

Most of our behaviors and responses become ingrained in our subconscious through repetition. We expect certain outcomes and see the world a certain way because that's what we have experienced in the past. And these patterns of experience, whether positive or negative, determine the way we react to the world. If the people we have encountered in the past were consistently kind, then we will expect new people to be kind as well. The flip side, of course, is also true: if people have generally been unreliable, we will react to others as if they will be unreliable, too.

When it comes to traumatic events, repetition isn't necessary to change the way we see and react to the world around us. The nervous system processes trauma differently than it does other stimuli. Because the intense, unresolved feelings of pain, fear, or doubt that trauma generates can overwhelm the conscious mind, the brain often represses these emotions as a protective mechanism, relegating them to the subconscious. Our neural pathways (the parts of the brain responsible for transmitting signals in the brain) become altered, profoundly changing how we perceive the world. This can cause us to view ordinary experiences through a lens of heightened fear and anxiety. We view every new situation through a trauma-influenced lens, constantly alert to threat or challenge. We're always assessing our surroundings to stay safe.

While repressing traumatic experiences spares the individual from ongoing emotional distress by temporarily burying these feelings until they can be safely processed, this unprocessed trauma may get "stored" or "stuck"—not just in our subconscious mind, but in our body. We develop habitual patterns rooted in the neural pathways that trauma has rewired. The result is a nervous system that is primed to overreact.

Fortunately, repetition offers a powerful tool for healing the subconscious mind, even from trauma. We can't control whether we experience trauma, but we *can* control our thoughts and actions. We can create new patterns of experience and new habits of thought that change our subconscious perceptions, by repeatedly engaging in specific actions or thoughts until they become automatic. By consistently applying and regularly repeating the healing techniques outlined in this book, we can apply the power of repetition to rewire our subconscious mind. This, in turn, helps calm the sensitive nervous system and restore balance to the five layers of energy, promoting overall well-being.

However, to ensure that this rewiring leads to genuine and enduring healing, it is crucial to address not just the subconscious mind but all of our layers of energy. Addressing only one layer of our being while neglecting others can lead to temporary relief, but it is rarely a permanent solution. It's akin to applying a Band-Aid to an infected wound. Talk therapy can help manage anxiety, but if the underlying cortisol levels and muscle tension are not addressed, the anxiety is likely to return. A massage might temporarily relieve muscle pain, but without tackling the sensitive nervous system's overactivity, the muscles are destined to tense up again.

It's important to rewire all layers of energy—our nervous system, organs and glands, muscles, emotions, and subconscious mind—to truly heal. A holistic approach prevents temporary fixes and ensures that the changes we make are lasting and meaningful.

To heal from trauma, we need to address the two key stress hormones—cortisol and adrenaline. But there's a third hormone that's crucial yet often overlooked in discussions about healing trauma and chronic stress. An imbalance in this hormone makes a sensitive nervous system further react and disrupts all five layers of energy. In the next chapter, I'll reveal this hormone and explore its pivotal role.

3

THE TRIFECTA EFFECT

Have you ever had one of those days where everything just feels right—you're in a good mood, feeling safe and happy—and then out of nowhere, you're blindsided by a wave of anxiety? It's confusing, because nothing in your environment has changed. There are no obvious stressors, no immediate threats. Yet there it is: a sudden, unexplained sense of anxiety that wraps around you like a cold wind. Your heart races, your breath shortens, and there's this unsettling feeling in the pit of your stomach, as if you're bracing for something to happen, even though everything is calm around you.

The reason is insulin—the third hormone that significantly impacts your sensitive nervous system.

During acute stress, adrenaline and cortisol prime the body for a fight-or-flight response. As we discussed in the last chapter, this means your heart rate increases and your muscles tense up. This fight-or-flight response also stimulates the release of something called glucagon—a hormone that elevates blood sugar levels—to provide the fuel the body needs to fight or flee. Glucagon, adrenaline, and cortisol elevate blood sugar levels by signaling the liver to transform stored glycogen into glucose (or sugar), a form of energy that the body's cells and tissues can use. When glucose enters the blood stream, the body uses insulin to move it into cells, where it can be used for fuel. During acute stress, however, insulin levels decrease. This keeps more glucose available in the bloodstream, where it can be quickly used by essential organs like the brain and muscles to respond to stress.

Typically, these hormones all return to homeostasis after a stress response. Stress hormones and glucagon levels decrease, the liver stops releasing glucose, and insulin levels return to normal. However, in individuals with a sensitive nervous system, stress hormones like cortisol remain elevated, continually signaling for more fuel. This promotes gluconeogenesis, an alternate process for creating glucose. Unlike during acute stress, when glucose is sourced from glycogen in the liver, gluconeogenesis creates glucose from noncarbohydrate sources like proteins, fats, and lactate, leading to an increased production of glucose.

In addition to promoting gluconeogenesis, cortisol also reduces glucose uptake by tissues, keeping more glucose available in the bloodstream. Normally, insulin helps to lower blood sugar and inhibits glucagon to prevent excess glucose production. Elevated cortisol levels override this inhibition, keeping blood sugar levels high. These persistently high glucose levels lead to an ongoing and excessive release of insulin—more than the body needs to transfer glucose from the blood into cells. Over days or weeks, this can result in hyperinsulinemia (excess insulin in the blood), which can cause blood sugar levels to drop rapidly, leading to hypoglycemia, or low blood sugar, causing internal stress.

The body releases adrenaline in response to this internal stress the same way it would for an external stressor. This, in turn, stimulates cortisol production, which triggers glucagon and gluconeogenesis to provide more fuel. The release of glucose in the blood stimulates insulin production again—which leads to hypoglycemia, which leads to the release of stress hormones, in a continuous loop.

This fluctuating pattern of blood sugar levels that swings from high to low intensifies the stress response and makes you feel tired, shaky, hungry, sweaty, and nervous. You reach for a quick energy boost, like candy, processed carbs, or caffeine, but these "quick fixes" just spike your blood sugar and set off the adrenaline, cortisol, and insulin cycle again—a phenomenon I refer to as the *Trifecta Effect*. Being trapped in this cycle doesn't just make you stressed and fatigued. It can also lead to unwanted weight gain, as low blood sugar prompts you to eat more high-calorie, low-nutrient foods, and low energy makes engaging in physical activity harder. Eventually, the Trifecta Effect leads to digestive, hormonal, and more serious health issues as well.

TRIFECTA EFFECT SYMPTOMS

All of the symptoms associated with a sensitive nervous system—including key indicators like fatigue, digestive issues, weight fluctuations, and stress or anxiety—stem from the Trifecta Effect of chronic stress or trauma. Now, this doesn't mean these issues are *always* linked to a sensitive nervous system. However, when I notice a combination of these symptoms alongside imbalances in the five layers of energy—tight hips or back pain, feeling overwhelmed in crowded spaces, burnout from a work ethic in overdrive paired with guilt over taking breaks—a sensitive nervous system is often the cause.

Digestion

In my years of coaching, I have never worked with someone with a sensitive nervous system who didn't have digestive issues. This is one of the main reasons people contact me for help.

You see, having a sensitive nervous system essentially means being "stuck" in fight, flight, or freeze mode, where the sympathetic nervous system is being continually activated. When the sympathetic nervous system is activated, its partner, the parasympathetic nervous system, cannot do its job. This system, also known as the "rest and digest" system, is responsible for calming the body, conserving energy, and overseeing processes like digestion and nutrient absorption. When we are constantly being diverted away from the parasympathetic system's restorative functions, it's easy to see how digestive issues can arise. Activation of the sympathetic nervous system prioritizes blood flow from the intestines to muscles and the brain to prepare for immediate action. This slows down the muscle movements in the intestines, which can halt peristalsis (the wave-like motion that propels food through the digestive tract) and lead to spasms that cause diarrhea or constipation. These muscle movements impede proper digestion.

Compounding this, chronic stress can, by decreasing the production of digestive juices and enzymes, cause stomach acid levels to be so low that protein isn't effectively broken down. This leads to a few potential problems. First, in a condition known as "leaky gut syndrome," undigested proteins enter the bloodstream, challenging the body and weakening the immune system. Second, undigested proteins reaching the small intestine can lead to bloating and gas, which, in turn, can result in conditions like small intestinal bacterial overgrowth (SIBO).[4] Finally, poor protein digestion can lead to deficiencies in essential nutrients like vitamin B12, iron, and zinc. These deficiencies can have significant impacts: low vitamin B12 levels can lead to anemia and neurological issues; iron deficiency can cause anemia and fatigue; and insufficient zinc can affect the immune system and skin health.

It's common for individuals, including many of my clients, to switch to a plant-based diet when they experience fatigue and discomfort after consuming meat, not realizing that the problem may be just that their bodies aren't producing sufficient stomach acid to properly digest the protein.

Interestingly, symptoms of low stomach acid can mimic those of high stomach acid, such as gastroesophageal reflux disease (GERD), where the muscle that acts as a doorway between the stomach and esophagus doesn't function correctly.

The Trifecta Effect's influence on stress and blood sugar instability, coupled with compromised digestion, naturally creates conditions favorable for fungal infections such as candidiasis, often referred to as candida overgrowth. Candida is a type of fungus typically found in small amounts in your mouth, skin, and intestines. It is a part of your body's normal microflora and an important contributor to your gut microbiome, a collection of beneficial bacteria, bad bacteria, yeast forms, and viruses that coexist in harmony to support healthy function. But when blood sugar levels are high—whether because of diet or the aftermath of a stress response—candida can multiply and potentially overrun the digestive tract, because it uses sugar as its primary food source. This excessive growth can escalate inflammation within the digestive system, manifesting in issues such as bloating, irritable bowel syndrome (IBS), and inflammatory bowel disease (IBD).[5] Where IBS is a syndrome characterized primarily by a combination of symptoms, such as abdominal pain, bloating, and diarrhea and/or constipation, caused by changes in the function of the digestive system, IBD is an umbrella term for two chronic inflammatory conditions—Crohn's disease and ulcerative colitis—that can cause severe complications such as ulcers and other damage to the digestive tract.

Anytime I teach my clients about candida overgrowth, their first reaction is to buy anti-fungal supplements. These supplements can be very helpful for short-term treatment, but when the root cause of the problem is an out-of-balance sensitive nervous system, they will never get rid of candida with supplements alone. The longer we avoid managing blood sugar, the more damage candida can do. Uncontrolled candida growth disrupts the gut microbiome. A disrupted gut microbiome weakens the immune system's ability to defend against pathogens, which can lead to serious infections throughout the body.[6] I call this *playing with fire*.

I don't know anyone who loves sugar more than me, and having to limit it or give it up was something I wasn't willing to do for a long time. Growing up, I always had athlete's foot, like really bad! I sometimes threw my socks away after a long day because of the terrible odor they had. As I got older, I developed fungus on my toes and oral thrush, and I was diagnosed with IBS. My sugar cravings were also through the roof (a candida overgrowth is known to cause sugar cravings). I found myself digging into the cabinet in the middle of the night looking for something sweet.

I spent thousands of dollars on the best programs, herbs, and supplements trying to beat persistent health issues related to candida overgrowth and the associated gut imbalances. Some supplements and herbs helped, but I could never fully overcome these issues. As soon as I came off the supplements, all of my symptoms returned. It was only after I learned how to balance my sensitive nervous system that I was able to overcome my candida overgrowth. Anytime I got out of balance, my candida overgrowth would return and give me problems. I lied to myself, convinced that it had nothing to do with me being out of balance. I'd spend more money on supplements and repeat the same ol' cycle. It wasn't until I realized I was jeopardizing my true aspirations in life that I decided I was done playing with fire. Recognizing and addressing the root cause of my digestive issues—the stress associated with a sensitive nervous system, influenced by lifestyle and dietary habits—and treating that cause was key to achieving genuine and lasting digestive health improvements.

Chronic Muscular Pain

When the nervous system is sensitive, it often overactivates the next layer of energy—the organs and glands—leading to an overproduction of stress hormones like cortisol. High levels of cortisol and the resultant stress response can trigger chronic inflammation within organs. Inflammation in any organ affects the third layer of energy—the muscular system—in a way that can lead to muscular imbalances. This happens because organs and glands share nerves with the muscles closest to them.[7]

Consider, for instance, inflammation in your digestive tract caused by constipation or by consuming foods that don't agree with you. When your intestines send an inflammation signal to the brain, it uses the same nerve pathway your core muscles do. When the brain receives this signal from your digestive tract, it can "turn off" or significantly weaken the core muscles, as it prioritizes managing the inflammation in your digestive system and redirects blood flow and other resources there. The body then compensates for this core muscle inhibition by overusing the hip flexors and lower back muscles. This can lead to muscle imbalances that impact posture and core strength and lead to various pains throughout the body, from the feet and ankles, to the knees, hips, and lower back, to the shoulders and neck. This shift in muscle use can cause a condition known as anterior pelvic tilt, characterized by the front of the pelvis dropping and the back rising. This tilt can exacerbate or contribute to further complications like increased lower back pain and reduced range of motion, and even impact gait and posture—something we'll talk about more in Chapter 5.

To bring this to life, consider my client Benji's situation: he was dealing with persistent knee and lower back pain. Despite engaging in corrective exercises specifically designed to address an anterior pelvic tilt, the pain persisted. The key to Benji's issue was his chronic digestive problems, which were weakening his core muscles and preventing the exercises from being effective. By focusing on his digestive health, we were able to restore balance to his muscular system and effectively correct the pelvic tilt, relieving his pain.

Insulin Resistance

Particularly when combined with an unhealthy lifestyle—a diet high in processed foods and sugars, coupled with a lack of regular physical activity—chronically elevated levels of stress hormones and increased blood sugar can also lead to insulin resistance, a condition in which the body's cells don't respond as effectively to insulin, making it harder for them to absorb glucose from the bloodstream. Insulin resistance occurs because, after a point, your cells have taken in as much glucose, stored as fat, as they can handle. It's like trying to pack more into an overstuffed suitcase—it just won't fit. So, with nowhere to go, the excess glucose remains in your bloodstream, keeping blood sugar levels high.

The liver, as one of the primary organs affected by our dietary choices and stress levels, is often the first to become insulin resistant. Under stress, our bodies are designed to release glucose into the bloodstream, providing energy for immediate use. The liver aids in this process by producing more glucose. When stress is constant, so is the liver's production of glucose, and, over time, this continuous output can cause the liver cells to become less sensitive to insulin.

This is particularly problematic because insulin is what signals the liver to stop releasing glucose into the blood. When the liver is exposed to high insulin levels continually due to ongoing stress, and so begins to ignore these signals, it just keeps producing glucose. This contributes to higher blood sugar levels and ultimately promotes insulin resistance in the rest of the body. The liver itself develops nonalcoholic fatty liver disease (NAFLD), one of the most common chronic liver disorders worldwide.[8]

As the liver becomes insulin resistant and progresses to NAFLD, its ability to produce bile acids is compromised. These acids are crucial for digesting and absorbing dietary fats in the small intestine. Without sufficient bile acids, dietary fats cannot be broken down effectively, leading to their malabsorption. This malabsorption affects the body's uptake of fat-soluble vitamins—such as A, K, E, and D—because these nutrients depend on the proper digestion of fats for their absorption. Consequently, a deficiency in bile production can lead to lower levels of these vital vitamins. Furthermore, the disruption of fat absorption can disturb the delicate balance of the gut, potentially leading to digestive disorders such as IBS.[9]

The pancreas then tries to make up for this inefficiency by increasing insulin production—and muscle, fat, and liver cells become even less responsive as a result. This ongoing cycle may result in metabolic syndrome, characterized by a variety of health issues such as high blood pressure, high triglycerides, polycystic ovary syndrome (PCOS), NAFLD, and obesity, among others.

Ultimately, improving insulin resistance involves managing our sensitive nervous system. By doing so, we can help our bodies respond better to insulin and break this challenging cycle.

THERE'S HOPE

Many people think the first step in slowing down the Trifecta Effect would be to focus on either adrenaline or cortisol, but that doesn't work. Most of my clients have either a therapist or counselor to help them reduce stress and deal with trauma or anxiety. They come to me because they are still struggling with fatigue, insulin resistance, and digestive issues. They are still stuck in the Trifecta Effect cycle.

Everyone experiences increases in adrenaline, cortisol, and insulin during acute stress, as the body's biological systems shift toward survival mode in the face of perceived threat. For those with a sensitive nervous system, it takes less stress to trigger this response, because their resting cortisol levels are typically higher than average. Imagine a cup nearly full: just a small addition can cause it to overflow. This easily triggered state means they can react more quickly and intensely to everyday stressors, leaving them feeling perpetually on edge, depleted of energy, and struggling with focus.

When clients come to me for holistic lifestyle coaching, overcoming stress is part of our goal. I design a program to help clients get clear on their goals, giving them small steps to create a less stressful life. I also design an exercise program that helps reduce stress through active meditation. You'll learn all these things, too, in this book. But the first step of the healing process is always breaking the Trifecta Effect, to ensure they have the energy they need to follow the program. And the only way to break the Trifecta Effect is to manage blood sugar. This is exactly how I helped my client Jeff overcome his anxiety, manage his digestive issues, and achieve weight loss.

Jeff is a financial advisor from Chicago who battled digestive and sleep issues, back pain, weight gain, and skin issues. Despite consulting various health professionals, he'd found no relief. Jeff was grinding away sixteen hours daily, glued to his desk.

The grind had brought him the life he'd always wanted: a house, a wife, and financial stability. But he wasn't taking the time to enjoy that life. I couldn't help but wonder why he kept pushing so hard.

Then it clicked: much like myself, he found it hard to relax and take a break. Why? Well, an unmanaged sensitive nervous system gives your brain the false perception that you are not safe. It keeps you preoccupied with potential threats, falling back on instinctual and automatic behaviors devoted to ensuring survival, and this continuous state of high alert drives you to push yourself harder than necessary. You operate under the belief that more success, more work, and more control will make you safer or more secure.

Jeff's relentless drive to achieve more was deeply rooted in the survival mindset he observed in his father from a young age. Growing up in an urban area, survival was a constant focus for Jeff and his family. His parents, immigrants from Africa, worked tirelessly to provide a better life for him and his siblings. But Jeff often felt lost in American culture and disconnected at school, where being different made it hard for him to fit in. He often struggled to grasp why his family faced difficulties providing basic necessities like food, shelter, and safety—challenges that didn't seem to affect some of his friends. He longed for his father's presence and assistance. But his father was constantly working, leading young Jeff to feel abandoned. These deep-seated feelings of abandonment carried over into his adulthood, fostering resentment toward his father. Interestingly, as an adult, Jeff found himself repeating a familiar pattern: always working. This commitment to work led him to inadvertently neglect his own health.

The first thing I addressed with Jeff was his nutrition. We improved his diet to stabilize his blood sugar levels, which helped manage insulin and was crucial for slowing down the Trifecta Effect. And not only did this help control his stress hormones, but it also made it easier for him to manage his appetite—something essential for consistent weight loss and avoiding overeating. With better nutrition leading to reduced stress, Jeff's digestion significantly improved. This set the stage for the next phase: introducing corrective exercises to address his muscle imbalances caused by an anterior pelvic tilt.

By focusing on stabilizing Jeff's blood sugar levels, which in turn regulated his insulin, we not only improved his energy and digestion but also significantly reduced his stress, making it easier for him to consistently adhere to his holistic program and stop procrastinating when it came to his health.

With more energy and less stress, Jeff now had the resilience and mental clarity needed to engage in deep healing work regarding his traumatic upbringing. Managing his sensitive nervous system empowered Jeff to forgive his father and make a conscious effort to spend more time with his loved ones as he prepared for fatherhood. Now, Jeff is a proud father to two daughters, and he has found a healthier work-life balance. He no longer spends his days glued to the computer but dedicates significant time to his family. Jeff's health improvements were just the beginning; the real transformation was in rewiring his mind, body, and emotions. And that was only possible because he was first able to take control of his blood sugar levels, calming his insulin surges and stopping the Trifecta Effect in its tracks.

4

BREAKING THE TRIFECTA EFFECT

My childhood was a time of continuous stress, shadowed by my mother's mental illness and drug addiction, abuse from her and her partners, and homelessness. Our situation was so bad that my father, despite suffering from severe arthritis in his hip that required a hip replacement he couldn't afford, had to sell his prescribed pain medication to afford motel stays for my younger brother and me. I vividly recall instances when my body reacted so intensely to external stressors that it was beyond my control. My stress manifested in shaking, a racing mind, rapid breathing, uncontrollable sweating, and extreme mood swings. I also battled numerous insecurities, from learning disabilities to being overweight, coupled with health challenges like digestive issues and relentless back and hip pain. "Hey, fat boy!" That taunt from my past, *fat boy*, still catches my attention, just like it did back then.

I knew my circumstances were anything but ordinary, and initially, I kept my struggles—both health and home life—to myself. In the urban community I hailed from, seeking help, whether it was consulting a doctor or talking to a counselor, was often stigmatized as a sign of weakness. I didn't want to be seen as "soft" by my peers.

As my issues intensified, I finally sought help. I visited doctors, spoke to a counselor, and opened up to my teachers and coaches. While the guidance from mentors and medical professionals was helpful—they did everything they could—I didn't find immediate solutions to my health problems, because the real challenge lay within myself. Struggling with consistency, I often fell into procrastination, becoming increasingly frustrated by my erratic energy levels and mood swings.

One day, I'd be full of inspiration and motivation, eager to improve in school, excel in sports, and maintain a positive outlook on my home life. The next day, I'd find myself unwilling to engage with my mentors and frustrated by my inability to concentrate—not just due to ADHD, but also because of brain fog and fatigue. This roller coaster of emotions and energy left me feeling trapped in a cycle of stress and anxiety, which increased my fear of never being good or intelligent enough to conquer my personal stress and trauma. Moreover, it heightened my dread of walking into the same trap other family members had: becoming homeless, falling into addiction, or turning to drug dealing as a means of survival.

Then, when I was in ninth grade, I discovered the transformative impact of managing my blood sugar.

At the time, I lived in a motel in front of the Holland Tunnel, an uncertain shelter I shared with my brother and father. This motel became a temporary home during the traumatic years of dealing with my mother's abuse, addiction, and eventual abandonment. During this time, I had two options. I could let the external stressors of being homeless, abused, and insecure bring me down, and succumb to my deepest fears of repeating my family's cycle of health problems, trauma, and poverty. Or, I could decide to change the paradigm. I could be the first one in my family to discover and address the root cause of their stress and health issues. I could become the first in my family to graduate from high school and pursue higher education, in hopes of not falling into the curse of generational poverty.

I decided to shift my family's paradigm.

Sitting on the motel bed, I opened my notebook, which also served as a journal, and sketched out a blueprint for my next step after middle school. That's when the idea of going to St. Anthony High School came to mind. They were known for their 100 percent college acceptance rate and renowned basketball program led by Hall of Fame Coach Bob Hurley Sr. My ambition crystallized: to earn a full basketball scholarship to St. Anthony as a stepping stone toward college.

I knew that, to reach my goal of being admitted into St. Anthony, I had to step up my game in academics. That was nonnegotiable. St. Anthony was a private institution celebrated for setting high standards both in the classroom and on the sports field. Managing my mood swings also became a priority; any slip-up could jeopardize my chances of getting crucial reference letters from my teachers. On the physical front, addressing my digestive issues and weight that contributed to my hip and back pain was imperative. These issues were direct obstacles to reaching my full athletic potential.

All of this meant being consistent about managing my mind, body, and emotions. The question was, how could I achieve this balance?

The revelation came after a recreational basketball game when I overheard St. Anthony's coaches remarking that I was talented but needed to shed some "baby fat." That moment was a wake-up call. Was losing weight all that stood between me and a scholarship at a school that almost guaranteed my acceptance to college? Back at the motel, I considered how to approach weight loss.

Curiously, I asked my dad, "Ay, dad, how do I lose this fat?" as I patted my belly.

His straightforward advice was "You have to burn more energy than you consume."

I reflected on my activity level; I was always on the move, playing basketball and walking to school to save bus fare. So I asked, "But how do I know how much energy I'm consuming?"

"Just check the nutritional facts, Pa"—what my dad calls me and my brothers. "It's about the calories, but also pay attention to the amount of sugar," he explained.

Equipped with this new insight, I used the motel's lobby computer to dive deeper into calorie research. I learned the importance of being in a caloric deficit—consuming fewer calories than I burned. This principle became my weight-loss strategy as I began my journey toward better health and athletic performance. I started closely monitoring my diet, particularly focusing on caloric intake.

However, I quickly encountered several obstacles, which I now know are common among individuals with a sensitive nervous system struggling with the Trifecta Effect: relentless hunger and sugar cravings; eating mindlessly or as a stress response or subconscious ritual; and an environment that did not encourage healthy eating habits.

Reducing my caloric intake immediately made me realize how constantly hungry I was; my sugar cravings seemed insatiable. And my environment wasn't very conducive to achieving my weight-loss goals. With my mother controlling our government-issued food stamps card and with income sporadic, dependent on my father selling his prescribed pain medication, meal options were unpredictable.

Often, by the time we had money on a given day, the only place still open was the Burger King behind the motel. Indulging in fries and a milkshake from Burger King had become a ritual for my brother Brandon and me. It was our way of subconsciously celebrating that we made it through another day. Junk food, and the comedy shows we watched while we ate it, allowed us to momentarily escape our daily stress and hardship.

After a few months of dedicating myself to counting calories, I had only managed to lose 5 pounds—a change that was barely noticeable. This wasn't so much a failure of the *calorie in versus calorie out* principle, but rather a struggle to avoid snacking that led to inconsistency in maintaining that caloric deficit. And despite shedding some weight, my belly fat persisted, as did my digestive issues and physical discomfort.

Then, one night, during a visit to Burger King, we discovered the ice cream machine was broken. Disappointed, especially since I had allocated my day's calories for that milkshake, I scanned the menu for alternatives. I decided to try something new—their Caesar salad with chicken.

Brandon and I returned to the motel, turned on the TV, and settled into our usual evening routine. As he opened his bag of fries, the aroma immediately made my mouth water, tempting me to ask for a few. But I knew Brandon was unlikely to share; he'd just remind me that he told me to get my own fries. Yet, something unexpected happened after I finished my salad and chicken. Brandon had fries left over, and for the first time, I didn't feel the urge to reach for them. I was completely satisfied after my meal.

That night, I experienced an unexpectedly good sleep and didn't wake up drenched in sweat as I usually did. The next morning, I felt remarkably different: no inflammation, the brain fog I was used to had lifted, and my mood was noticeably more stable. I realized that my dinner choice might have contributed to this positive change. Intrigued and a bit puzzled, I used the motel's computer before school to search for information about the connections between nutrition, particularly sugar, and mental, physical, and emotional health. But all I found were statements like "Sugar is necessary for energy," and "The amount of sugar doesn't matter for weight loss as long as you're in a caloric deficit." None of these sources addressed the connections I was beginning to suspect.

I began to doubt myself, thinking that, as a nonexpert, I must be mistaken about what I was experiencing. But, trusting my intuition, I continued to reduce my sugar intake, sometimes cutting sugar out completely—especially processed sugar. This significantly improved my mental, physical, and emotional well-being. I managed to lose all the excess body weight, alleviate my digestive and physical pain, and develop a newfound consistency in my mood. I had broken the Trifecta Effect.

Despite the ongoing stress from events outside of my control, from the abuse I endured at home with my mother to the hardships of being homeless and living in a hotel, I found myself equipped with a powerful tool to tackle these stressors that I'd never had before—*energy*. The guidance I had been receiving from my mentors started to truly resonate, enhancing my academic efforts. And my dedication and hard work paid off when I secured a full basketball scholarship at St. Anthony and participated in Bob Hurley's acclaimed basketball program. Eventually, I transitioned to playing football and earned a full scholarship to college. I became the first Division I football player in St. Anthony's history.

Even when we find ourselves at the mercy of external stressors over which we have little control, we can at least manage our internal stressors. We can maintain our blood sugar levels through mindful dietary choices, preventing stress hormone fluctuations from snowballing. Achieving this unlocks a reservoir of energy that empowers us to take command of our mind, body, and emotions and allows us to maintain focus on our goals. It lets us heal trauma and chronic stress. It lets us achieve goals no one in our family has ever achieved before. It helps us move forward and break free from the emotional confines of always feeling unsafe and being in survival mode.

The remarkable outcomes I experienced early on were just the beginning. Maintaining my energy allowed me to leverage my full football scholarship at Delaware State University into studying movement science, nutrition, physical therapy, and strength and conditioning and graduating with a Bachelor of Science.

I also acquired multiple nutritional certifications after graduating college, and the young boy once torn between his intuition and what the experts were saying achieved his grand ambition of becoming an "expert" himself. Now, when someone yells, "Ay, fat boy," I no longer feel the need to look over my shoulder. The journey has led me to a place of confidence and purpose, far removed from the insecurities of my past.

Now, it's your turn to take on this kind of transformative journey.

We frequently set ambitious goals; maybe you already have some yourself. But without consistent energy, particularly when navigating a sensitive nervous system, we become overwhelmed and reactive and, despite our best intentions, find ourselves procrastinating on our goals and doubting our ability to achieve them. The problem isn't a lack of willpower or a "weak" mindset. It's a lack of energy. The first step to moving forward in your own life is achieving sustainable energy, and achieving sustainable energy means breaking the Trifecta Effect.

PULLING THE STRINGS OF STRESS

As we saw in Chapter 3, traumatic experiences often embed themselves deep within our subconscious, surfacing as overreactions to acute stress and giving rise to what we know as a sensitive nervous system. This heightened sensitivity prompts an overproduction of stress hormones—namely cortisol and adrenaline—which, in turn, trigger insulin surges and lead to blood sugar fluctuations. These fluctuations then become additional stressors, perpetuating the cycle by driving the production of even more cortisol, adrenaline, and insulin.

We saw how adrenaline and cortisol release from stress can lead to increases in blood sugar, either as part of the normal, healthy stress response or as the result of a sensitive nervous system. But blood sugar levels also increase as a result of diet.

Here's how it works: consuming high-glycemic foods—foods that spike your blood sugar quickly, such as white bread, sugary drinks, or processed snacks—lead to significant spikes in blood sugar. This is especially true when you eat these foods on their own, without consuming enough protein and dietary fats. When a lot of glucose hits the bloodstream all at once, the body releases a large amount of insulin to handle the sudden influx. However, this rapid release of insulin can often be more than what is necessary, known as an overreaction. These blood sugar spikes are then

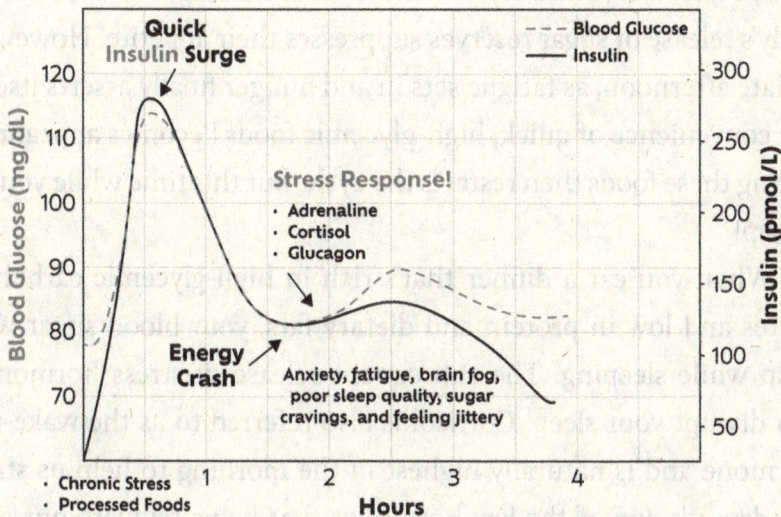

Chronic stress and processed food consumption lead to a rapid rise and subsequent crash in both blood glucose and insulin levels (represented by the black and gray curves). This crash is associated with symptoms such as anxiety, fatigue, and brain fog that can hinder your healing journey.

quickly followed by sharp dips, and these dips trigger the body's response to stress, releasing adrenaline and cortisol.

Adrenaline, cortisol, and glucagon prompt the liver to convert glycogen (stored glucose) into usable sugar, which is then released into the bloodstream. The excessive amount of insulin still in the blood from the original spike in blood sugar quickly shuttles this glucose into the body's cells for immediate energy use . . . or, if the energy isn't needed, storage as glycogen. This creates another sudden drop in blood sugar levels, perpetuating the cycle. This process can contribute to increased fat storage in the body.

These stress-induced blood sugar fluctuations, whether due to an unmanaged sensitive nervous system or eating high-glycemic foods, can lead to irregular eating patterns. Many people find themselves skipping meals during the day: stress hormones might keep them overly alert and busy, which makes them forget to eat, or their body's release of sugar reserves suppresses their appetite. However, by late afternoon, as fatigue sets in and hunger finally asserts itself, the convenience of quick, high-glycemic foods becomes appealing. Eating these foods then restarts the cycle, but this time while you're asleep!

When you eat a dinner that's rich in high-glycemic carbohydrates and low in protein and dietary fats, your blood sugar will drop while sleeping. The subsequent release of stress hormones can disrupt your sleep. Cortisol is also referred to as the wake-up hormone and is naturally highest in the morning to help us start the day; it's one of the key hormones that helps regulate our circadian rhythm, our internal clock that cycles between sleepiness and alertness at regular intervals. The other key hormone that affects our circadian rhythm is melatonin, which is known as the sleep hormone; it signals that it's time for rest. Ideally, when cortisol is high, melatonin should be low. When melatonin is high, then cortisol should be low. An imbalance between these two, as when a high-glycemic snack leads to a blood sugar crash and cortisol release at night, affects sleep. My clients commonly experience sleep disturbances due to stress hormone fluctuations. They might struggle to fall asleep, wake up between one and four in the morning, need to get up often during the night to urinate, or experience night sweats.

This can make mornings a struggle, and so many reach for coffee or other pick-me-ups. However, this can kick off stress hormones again (see the section on caffeine on page 52) and keep this cycle going. And remember, having a sensitive nervous system will make this cycle occur faster.

What about people who don't skip meals during the day? Sometimes the problem isn't how much someone eats or doesn't eat during the day, but *what* they eat. They might start the day by whipping up a healthy breakfast like a fruit smoothie, toast, and a boiled egg. But two to three hours later, they feel drained, jittery, hungry, and anxious. To combat this blood sugar dip, they might grab candy, junk food, or coffee. These quick boosts work in the short term but shoot up their blood sugar and speed up the Trifecta Effect cycle.

Why does this happen? It's something I needed clarification on during my healing journey, too. Anytime I ate healthy meals similar to the one mentioned above, I felt tired, hungry, and craved sugar all day. I eventually gained weight because I couldn't stop snacking and was too tired to exercise. And yes, smoothies, toast, and a boiled egg can be considered healthy. But for you and me, with our sensitive nervous systems, we have to consider not only the individual foods we eat, but also the macronutrient ratio of our meals.

THE BIG THREE

Before we delve deep into the macronutrient ratio your sensitive nervous system needs, let's first look at what macronutrients are. Macronutrients, often referred to simply as *macros*, are the building blocks of our diet. They're the primary sources of the energy for our body. We need a balance of all three macronutrients to function optimally, because each plays a unique and essential role in our health and well-being. These nutrients are broken down into three main categories: carbohydrates, proteins, and fats.

Carbohydrates give us a quick energy boost to fuel our muscles and brain. Protein is essential for repairing and building all body tissues, from our muscles to our hair. Fats, which are often misunderstood, are crucial for supporting cell growth, protecting our organs, and aiding in the absorption of certain nutrients. Getting the right balance of these macronutrients not only provides the energy we need to power our daily activities but also helps us stabilize our blood sugar, and our nervous system as a whole, by avoiding spikes.

Consuming too many carbohydrates with insufficient protein and healthy fats leads to blood sugar spikes that drive the Trifecta Effect. Proteins and fats are essential in moderating how quickly sugar is absorbed into the bloodstream. When you eat a meal rich in protein and fats, these nutrients interact with carbohydrates to slow down the digestion process. This slower digestion means that glucose is released more gradually into your bloodstream, helping to prevent the sharp peaks and dips in blood sugar levels that can trigger a stress response in the body. By maintaining the right balance of macronutrients, we ensure steadier blood sugar levels and a more stable internal environment.

The breakfast example mentioned earlier is predominantly carbohydrates (the toast, the fruits in the smoothie), with low amounts of protein and fats (the egg). As a result, you might find yourself feeling hungry only two or three hours later, because your body processes these sugars quickly and your blood sugar plummets.

This does not mean you should go on a ketogenic (or keto) diet, which is predominantly high in fats, with moderate protein and very low carbohydrates. Even though I know people who benefited from this diet, I don't follow it, and neither do my clients. The important part is to ensure you get sustainable sources of energy and feel satiated. Including sources of protein and healthy fats in the smoothie, for example, such as a scoop of protein powder and a tablespoon of nut butter, can help significantly. With more protein and fats, the absorption of sugar into the bloodstream is slowed down, keeping you fuller for longer—and soothing your sensitive nervous system.

My program emphasizes that healing is a journey, not a quick fix. We're striving for progress, not perfection. Diets with many restrictions often have a short-lived impact because they are hard to maintain. While some people choose to stick to strict diets to address specific health concerns or achieve a particular goal, restrictive diets can be stressful for people dealing with trauma and frequent stress responses. Instead of restricting carbohydrates, we focus on managing them wisely—choosing whole, nutrient-dense foods that provide steady energy and support overall wellness.

MACRONUTRIENTS FOR HEALTH AND STRESS RELIEF

Protein plays a pivotal role in counteracting the Trifecta Effect. That's why it's the first macronutrient I focus on when working with clients. I've noticed that many of my clients don't consume enough protein throughout the day and instead rely heavily on processed foods to meet their energy needs.

Protein has a small effect on blood glucose levels and won't create a big spike in blood sugar. In fact, protein helps prevent blood sugar spikes by blunting the absorption of carbohydrates. A lack of sufficient protein in your diet doesn't just make stabilizing blood sugar levels harder. It also increases the likelihood that you'll frequently snack and overindulge in junk food.[10]

Protein plays a key role in regulating our appetite by suppressing ghrelin, the hormone responsible for signaling hunger to our brains. Additionally, protein has a high thermic effect, meaning it requires more energy for digestion, absorption, and metabolization compared to fats and carbohydrates. This increased metabolic demand helps burn more calories, making protein a crucial component in weight management and metabolic health.

After increasing protein intake, we shift our attention to replacing processed carbohydrates with fruits and vegetables. Most American adults do not meet the recommended intake for fruits and vegetables. A staggering *90 percent* fall short.[11]

Fruits and vegetables are important for a few reasons. The big one is that they are rich in fiber, which, like protein, helps stabilize blood sugar by preventing sudden blood sugar spikes and the resulting dips that trigger a stress response. Foods with high fiber content, especially fruits and vegetables, are typically low on the glycemic index, which means they cause a slower and more stable rise in blood sugar.

Fiber also feeds the beneficial bacteria in our guts. A diet dominated by processed carbohydrates and lacking fruits and vegetables can lead to dysbiosis, where harmful bacteria outnumber beneficial bacteria in the digestive tract. This sets the stage for conditions like the candida overgrowth we discussed in Chapter 3. Feeding the beneficial bacteria in your digestive tract with soluble fiber can assist with repairing this bacterial imbalance.

Finally, we turn to the third macronutrient, fat.

In the Western world, we often have an imbalanced relationship with fats, particularly when it comes to omega fatty acids, a crucial type of fat our bodies need for various functions. About one hundred years ago, people ate a balanced ratio of omega-6s, which are essential for cell membrane integrity and support inflammation as part of the body's healing process, and omega-3s, which counteract inflammation and support heart and brain health, at around 4:1 or even less.[12] This balance was the natural result of a diet rich in whole foods, fish, and plant oils, which naturally contain both omega-6 and omega-3 fatty acids in ratios that promote health. For instance, a meal might have included fish (a good source of omega-3), served alongside a salad dressed with olive oil (which has a balanced omega-6 to omega-3 ratio), providing an overall dietary fat intake close to the ideal 4:1 ratio.

The ratio in today's typical Western diet, in contrast, leans heavily toward 20:1 in favor of omega-6, or *five times* more omega-6 than in the recommended 4:1 ratio. To visualize what a 20:1 diet looks like, consider a day of meals predominantly featuring fried foods cooked in vegetable oils, snacks like chips and cookies, and minimal omega-3-rich foods like fish or flaxseeds. This skewed ratio contributes to increased inflammation—which triggers the release of stress hormones, intensifying the Trifecta Effect.

The goal is to balance your omega-6 to omega-3 ratio. This can be achieved by taking omega-3 supplements, incorporating fatty fish (like salmon) into your diet at least twice a week, and reducing your intake of foods high in omega-6. That means avoiding processed vegetable oils like corn, soybean, canola, safflower, and sunflower, as well as foods containing these oils. Instead, I recommend my clients incorporate healthy fats into their diets, such as olive and coconut oil, avocados, nuts, seeds, and fatty fish.

BREAKING THE TRIFECTA EFFECT

Combining protein with low-glycemic fruits and vegetables and healthy fats will help manage your blood sugar. Doing so allows you to avoid the blood sugar spikes and dips created by either stress or a diet that's deficient in protein and fiber and high in sugar and the wrong kind of fats. Your goal is to ensure each of your meals has enough protein, fiber, and healthy fats.

Let's go back to the breakfast example we discussed earlier in this chapter: a smoothie, toast, and a boiled egg. If we were to add some avocado to the toast, trade the boiled egg for three scrambled eggs, and make sure the smoothie was made with low-glycemic fruits and vegetables like berries and spinach and some protein, like a nut butter or scoop of protein powder, the mix of macronutrients would mean a more balanced rise in blood sugar that doesn't trigger a stress response.

After years of trial and error, I found I still had some blood sugar dips even when applying this new dietary approach. I began to delve deeper into the nature of carbohydrates and their effect on the body. I discovered that, surprisingly, not all carbohydrates behaved the same way within my system. While some, like the simple sugars in fruits, provided a steady release of energy when paired with proteins and fats, starch-heavy foods like bread and pasta would consistently lead to fluctuations in my blood sugar levels.

This is also true for many of my clients. Give it a try yourself while making adjustments in your protein, carbohydrate, and fat intake. Notice if you still have an energy dip after consuming starchy carbohydrates. If so, try cutting out starches for three days and see if your digestion, energy, stress, and sleep improve. If so, you may, like me, be very sensitive to starchy carbohydrates and want to limit your intake.

IGNORING DEHYDRATION FUELS STRESS

What you eat is important, but so is what you drink. Staying hydrated is important because stress and dehydration compound each other, creating a challenging loop.[13] When we're stressed, our fight-or-flight response can lead to symptoms like a faster heart rate, nausea, tiredness, or headaches—and interestingly, these are also signs of dehydration. Stress can lead to dehydration by diverting blood away from the kidneys and slowing down the hydration process. And dehydration itself can trigger a stress response because the body sees it as a threat to its functioning.

Drinking more water throughout your day can help break this cycle. Generally, aim to drink about half to a full ounce of water for each pound you weigh daily. So, if you're 150 pounds, you'd shoot for 75 to 150 ounces of water daily. If you're active and live in a hot climate, lean toward the higher end. If you're more sedentary and live in a cooler environment, you might need less.

CAFFEINE WARNING

As we explore the nuances of breaking the Trifecta Effect, it's essential to address the potent role caffeine plays in this dynamic. Caffeine, a familiar stimulant found in coffee, tea, and many energy drinks, can significantly influence your nervous system and blood sugar levels.

Caffeine mimics the body's stress response, triggering the release of adrenaline that leads to increased cortisol production. This can exacerbate the Trifecta Effect, particularly when caffeine is consumed in large quantities or on an empty stomach, without food to slow its absorption. Beyond these immediate effects, caffeine's ability to disrupt your sleep cycle makes healing from stress more challenging. A restless night induced by late caffeine consumption can unsettle your nervous system, leaving it more susceptible to stress. And poor sleep can also lead to blood sugar imbalances the following day.

To manage caffeine's potent effects and prevent the overstimulation of the nervous system, it's important to take a multifaceted approach:

- Moderation is key—if you're accustomed to several cups of coffee or tea throughout the day, gradually reduce your intake.
- Be mindful of timing; consuming caffeine late in the day can disrupt your sleep cycle, potentially leaving you prone to stress and blood sugar imbalances and a restless nervous system.
- Pair caffeine with a balanced meal or snack rich in protein and healthy fats to slow the absorption of caffeine into the bloodstream and provide a more sustained energy release.
- Increase water intake to counteract caffeine's dehydrating effects.
- Consider exploring caffeine-free alternatives, like herbal teas or decaffeinated coffee, which can reduce overall caffeine intake while preserving the comfort of a warm beverage ritual.

By adopting these practices, you can still enjoy the benefits of caffeine while minimizing its role in initiating the Trifecta Effect.

MEASURE TO MASTER: YOUR HEALTH PROGRESS DIARY

People often raise their eyebrows when I discuss prioritizing nutrition as the first step in breaking the Trifecta Effect. My response? "Don't just take my word for it; give it a shot and see the results firsthand." That's the same attitude I encourage you to adopt. As you tweak your diet, monitor the following areas, observing any positive changes during your journey.

Grab a fresh journal and a pen that feels good to write with (there's something uniquely satisfying about putting thoughts down with a pen that glides effortlessly on paper!). In your journal, dedicate the left side to tracking the items below and reserve the right side for exercises that I'll introduce to you later in this book. Track your progress each day.

Use a scale from 1 to 10 for each item below, where 1 indicates you felt very dissatisfied or had a negative experience, and 10 indicates you felt highly satisfied or had a positive experience.

- Stress: On a scale of 1 to 10, how stressed did you feel today, with 1 being very stressed and 10 being not stressed at all?
- Anxiety: On a scale of 1 to 10, how calm were you today, with 1 being very anxious and 10 being completely calm?
- Bowel Movements: On a scale of 1 to 10, how comfortable and regular were your bowel movements?
- Bloating: On a scale of 1 to 10, how bloated did you feel after your meals today, with 1 being extremely bloated and 10 being not bloated at all?
- Energy: On a scale of 1 to 10, how energetic did you feel today?
- Sleep: On a scale of 1 to 10, how restful was your sleep last night?

Regaining Your Rhythm: Your Balance Checklist

If you find your scores dipping, use this checklist to pinpoint potential areas you might've missed:

1. Have you incorporated protein in every meal?
2. Did you consume adequate fruits, vegetables, and fiber throughout your day?
3. Have you had enough water today?

EAT TO HEAL

With the nutritional approach in this chapter, we not only regulate our internal stress responses but also start the process of rewiring the first layer of energy—the nervous system. This helps us handle external stressors that we can't predict or control in a calmer way. This way of eating prevents sudden drops in blood sugar that make us feel stressed, improves digestion, stops us from overeating, and aids in weight management. With the additional energy and focus, we're better prepared to use the advice we receive from professionals and follow the steps in this book to heal.

Learning about blood sugar's role in regulating energy was eye-opening during my healing journey. My unstable blood sugar, caused by stress and poor nutrition, amplified my stress and triggered subconscious responses created from trauma. Understanding the impact of what I was eating was a significant breakthrough on my journey to overcoming stress and trauma. No longer was stress a trigger, as I now had the patience and energy necessary for counseling and tutoring—resources that were instrumental in overcoming my trauma and learning disabilities. And that understanding has since become a cornerstone of my approach to holistic health coaching.

While stabilizing your blood sugar is crucial for managing internal stressors, it's only the first step. The next is applying foundational holistic healing steps that can lead to significant improvements in sleep, digestion, and physical pain. Stabilizing blood sugar does more than just manage stress and improve energy—it lays the groundwork for healing the five layers of energy.

5

HEALING MIND AND BODY

Before I understood my sensitive nervous system, I struggled with weight problems, digestive issues, and physical pain. I was similar to those I coach, spending my last dollar on the latest supplement that promised to help with my digestive issues, believing that sleep was not as important as working harder to survive, and thinking that if my exercise program didn't make me sweat and nearly pass out, it wasn't effective. I now understand how I oversimplified the complex relationship between the mind and body, not taking into account how stress and lifestyle choices impact overall health, and how that oversimplification prevented me from reaching my goals. Once I started managing my stress and made healthier choices, the weight came off, my digestive issues cleared up, and the physical pain disappeared. These changes didn't take years—they started to happen right away, as soon as I began breaking the Trifecta Effect and focusing on healing one layer of energy at a time.

Now it's your turn. Once you've broken the Trifecta Effect, you can apply the energy you've gained to retraining your mind, body, and emotions. In this chapter are the most effective, practical ways to rewire the five layers of energy and strengthen the mind-body connection. These represent foundational steps on the path to holistic healing because they each address the root causes of imbalances related to a sensitive nervous system. Addressing these root causes quickly leads to noticeable improvements, helping you feel better physically and mentally. As you integrate these practices into your daily life, you'll notice increased energy, reduced stress, less physical pain, and an overall sense of balance and well-being.

HEALING WITH SLEEP

The better your night's rest, the more beneficial it is for your nervous system. Insomnia affects an estimated 33 percent of adults seen in medical family practice offices and has long-term and serious effects on health, including increased risk of heart disease, diabetes, high blood pressure, depression, increased stress, and insulin resistance.[14]

Much like other habits, not resting can become a subconscious pattern, particularly for those with a sensitive nervous system. A sensitive nervous system's constant state of alertness, driven by heightened levels of cortisol and adrenaline, dulls your body's rest signals, as adrenaline masks your fatigue. Since cortisol counteracts the action of melatonin—the hormone that promotes sleep—achieving restful sleep becomes a challenge.

Alleviating your internal and external stressors to manage stress hormones is an important part of supporting sleep, but there are other factors to be aware of to ensure a good night's rest. Maintaining a consistent sleep schedule is essential, but eating enough protein, healthy fats, and low-glycemic carbohydrates before bed, as we learned in Chapter 4, is also crucial. Additionally, creating healthy boundaries in your home environment to promote relaxation and reduce stress is important, which we will delve into in more detail in Chapter 7.

Addressing the Trifecta Effect through nutrition, as outlined in Chapter 4, prevents disturbances caused by stress hormones released in response to blood sugar fluctuations during sleep. As we saw in that chapter, unstable blood sugar levels can cause blood sugar to drop during sleep, which triggers the release of cortisol. Increased levels of cortisol cause melatonin levels to decrease, and this imbalance between your stress and sleep hormones disrupts your sleep. You might find yourself waking up between one and four in the morning, struggling to fall back asleep, frequently getting up during the night to urinate, or experiencing night sweats. By consuming a dinner rich in protein, healthy fats, and low-glycemic carbohydrates, you can avoid these sleep disturbances.

Cortisol is released in response to light, and typically peaks between 6 and 9 AM, coinciding with sunrise. In other words, exposure to light increases stress hormones. Cortisol isn't in itself a bad thing. It is essential for our daily functioning; it provides the energy we need to start our day, helps with regulating our metabolism, reduces inflammation, and controls the body's sleep-wake cycle.

But when we are exposed to light at the wrong time—for example, from your cell phone screen while lying in bed or keeping the TV on while drifting off to sleep—our brain and hormonal systems react as though it were morning, releasing cortisol and kickstarting the Trifecta Effect cycle . . . even if you had a dinner that stabilizes blood sugar.

Caffeine, tobacco, and medications that stimulate the central nervous system (such as Adderall or Ritalin), as well as vigorous exercise before bed, can also contribute to sleep disturbances. These activities excite the sympathetic nervous system and signal to the brain that it's time to wake up, even as you're trying to go to sleep.

A useful guideline for caffeine consumption is to have your last serving before 3 PM, though you may find you personally need to stop sooner (or can stop later) than this. Caffeine has a half-life of about five hours, meaning it takes that long for half of it to be processed by the body. Provided you haven't consumed excessive amounts, ending your caffeine intake by mid-afternoon should let most of it clear your body by bedtime. Regarding tobacco and certain medications, it's best to consult your primary care provider for tailored advice.

HEALING WITH GUT-FRIENDLY EATING

Most of the clients I've worked with who have a sensitive nervous system live with chronic gut and digestive issues, which is not a surprise to me. If you recall the insights from Chapter 2, we know having a sensitive nervous system essentially means being "stuck" in fight, flight, or freeze mode, where the sympathetic nervous system is continually activated. The sympathetic nervous system works in opposition to the parasympathetic nervous system, which helps us feel calm and stimulates digestion. When the sympathetic nervous system is activated, it can suppress the parasympathetic nervous system, disrupting our ability to digest food properly.

When we follow the nutritional approach to breaking the Trifecta Effect, we assist the nervous system in shifting from fight, flight, or freeze to "rest and digest." This is a crucial first step. However, once the nervous system has returned to calm, we still need to rebuild the microbiome and create new eating habits. When we do, we not only heal the gut but also, as you'll see on page 64, take the first step toward overcoming chronic muscular pain.

Restoring Gut Balance

The quickest way to improve your gut health—to support your microbes, heal from dysbiosis, and rebuild the integrity of your gut wall—is to add fermented foods, such as sauerkraut, yogurt, kefir, and kimchi, to your diet. These foods are rich in naturally occurring probiotics, beneficial bacteria that help maintain the natural balance of organisms in your intestines. They play a key role in supporting digestion, boosting the immune system, and preventing the growth of harmful bacteria. Probiotics are particularly important after experiencing conditions like dysbiosis, leaky gut, or candida overgrowth, as these issues involve disruption of the gut's ecosystem. Fermented foods not only help replenish the gut's beneficial bacteria but also enhance nutrient absorption and reduce inflammation, promoting overall gut health.

When you start to incorporate fermented foods into your diet, it's important to go slowly to allow your gut to adjust. Begin with small amounts, such as a spoonful of sauerkraut or a few sips of kefir, and gradually increase your intake over time. This gradual introduction helps prevent any potential digestive discomfort. For more detailed guidance, you can find more resources at www .begreatwithnate.com.

Mindful Eating for Gut Health

I love to ask one particular question whenever a client reaches out to me for coaching, and now, I want to ask you: Do you chew your food thoroughly while eating?

Think about the last meal you had. Did you chew your food until it was liquefied, or did you take two big bites and swallow quickly before taking the next one? If your answer is "Oh my God, no, I never chew my food thoroughly!" you're not alone. This, too, is connected to having a sensitive nervous system. Subconsciously, we become so used to rushing to the next thing on our to-do list that we don't take the time to be present with our food. We are more concerned with safety and security than with nourishing ourselves.

Chewing our food is the first step in digestion. The more we chew our food, the more it mixes with our saliva, which contains digestive enzymes that begin breaking down carbohydrates right in the mouth. Proper chewing also signals the rest of the digestive system to prepare for incoming food, which allows our body to absorb more nutrients and makes digestion easier.

So, next time you eat, make a conscious effort to slow down, chew well, and give your body the care it deserves. Aim to chew each bite around twenty to thirty times, until the food is liquefied.

Reducing Inflammation and Bloating

You saw in Chapter 2 the power of holistic healing: how the five layers of energy play a significant role in healing from trauma and rewiring the mind and body. Breaking the Trifecta Effect begins to heal the first layer of energy—the nervous system. With better stress management, the organs and glands involved in digestion—the second layer of energy—can better digest and assimilate the nutrients from your food. Just as the first layer of energy impacts the second, improving digestion is the first step to healing the third layer of energy, the muscular system.

When the digestive system becomes inflamed, the nerves associated with it send out chemical messages to the brain that there is irritation or inflammation in the digestive tract. As explained in Chapter 3, the core muscles (the group of muscles surrounding your internal organs, spine, and hips) share the same nerve pathways as the digestive tract. And since the organs and glands are more essential for survival than the muscular system, the nervous system reallocates resources like blood flow from the muscular system to the digestive tract to help with inflammation. A muscle lacking blood circulation cannot contract properly, which means it doesn't function well. The muscles weaken. Reduced blood flow also affects peristalsis, the involuntary constriction and relaxation of muscles in the digestive tract, slowing down the transit of food, increasing gas, and causing bloating and discomfort.[15]

The good news is that, by following the nutritional protocol in Chapter 4, adding fermented foods, and chewing your food until it's liquefied, you can heal digestion and send fewer inflammatory signals to the brain. This restores blood flow to the core muscles, allowing them to function properly and reducing bloating. My clients love reporting back to me when their bloating is gone, and I love hearing this update because it also indicates they are ready for the next step in their healing process: healing the muscular system.

HEALING CHRONIC MUSCULAR PAIN

I haven't yet coached a client with a sensitive nervous system who didn't have chronic muscular pain and stiffness, particularly in the hips, back, knees, and feet. This, too, is related to trauma. As detailed in Chapter 2, during traumatic experiences or persistent chronic stress, your body shifts into a heightened state of alertness that prepares you for either confronting the threat or making a swift escape. This physiological response includes tightening your psoas muscles—deep hip flexors—to stabilize and protect your spine while preparing your body for rapid movement, which pulls your pelvis forward in a position called anterior pelvic tilt.

The body is equipped with numerous reflexes to react to external stimuli without needing direct brain intervention. When you touch a hot surface, for example, your hand quickly and involuntarily pulls back—an action that's facilitated by reflex pathways. These pathways are mediated by the spinal cord, the hub of the central nervous system. In stressful scenarios, signals from the brain travel through the spine to initiate this reflexive contraction of the psoas muscles and alter posture.

In normal circumstances, when the stress has passed, the muscles release. But trauma can embed this tightness in the psoas muscles by subconsciously keeping them contracted. Especially when stress is prolonged or frequently triggered (and when physical activity does not dissipate the tension in these muscles), this ongoing muscle contraction can lead to imbalances that cause discomfort or pain. This pain further negatively impacts posture.

Your psoas muscles connect your hips to your lumbar spine or lower back. In an anterior pelvic tilt, overly tight psoas muscles rotate your hips forward and increase the curvature of your lower back. This position causes a chain reaction in the rest of your body.

ANTERIOR PELVIC TILT

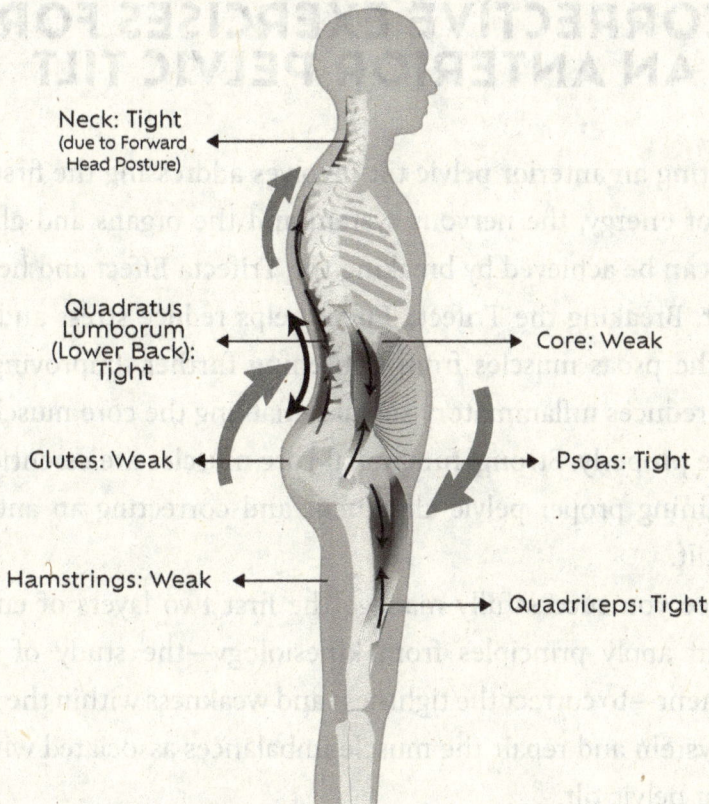

Neck: Tight
(due to Forward
Head Posture)

Quadratus
Lumborum
(Lower Back):
Tight

Core: Weak

Glutes: Weak

Psoas: Tight

Hamstrings: Weak

Quadriceps: Tight

The common muscular imbalances associated with an anterior pelvic tilt, including tight psoas and quadriceps muscles and weak core, glutes, and hamstrings.

Your shoulders rotate inward, which pulls your head forward and places stress on the trapezius and neck muscles, leading to slumping or slouching. An anterior pelvic tilt also shifts your body weight forward as you walk and move, which increases pressure on your knees, calves, and feet. Your quadriceps tense up, and this tightness spreads to the adductors, the muscles in your groin. Over time, this domino effect leads to muscle and joint pain all over your body.

CORRECTIVE EXERCISES FOR AN ANTERIOR PELVIC TILT

Correcting an anterior pelvic tilt involves addressing the first two layers of energy, the nervous system and the organs and glands, which can be achieved by breaking the Trifecta Effect and healing the gut. Breaking the Trifecta Effect helps reduce stress and prevents the psoas muscles from tightening further. Improving gut health reduces inflammatory signals, enabling the core muscles to activate properly. Strong, functional core muscles are essential for maintaining proper pelvic alignment and correcting an anterior pelvic tilt.

Once you successfully manage the first two layers of energy, you can apply principles from kinesiology—the study of body movement—to correct the tightness and weakness within the muscular system and repair the muscle imbalances associated with an anterior pelvic tilt.

When your psoas muscles are chronically tight, and your core muscles are weakened due to stress and inflammation, this response becomes subconsciously wired into your reflex pathways. By correcting muscle imbalances, you can rewire these pathways. The more consistent you are in addressing an anterior pelvic tilt through stress management and a corrective exercise program, the more these practices become ingrained in your subconscious, supporting the emergence of the new you.

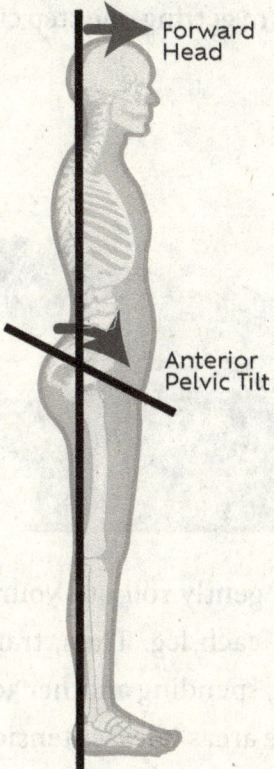
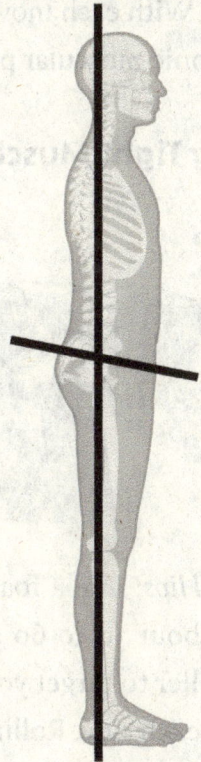

BAD POSTURE

Forward
Head

Anterior
Pelvic Tilt

Old You

GOOD POSTURE

New You

The left profile illustrates poor posture characterized by a forward head and a pronounced anterior pelvic tilt. The right profile demonstrates correct posture with a neutral spine alignment and showcases the ideal spine, pelvis, and leg positioning for balanced posture.

It is essential to target both tight and weak muscles to heal chronic muscular pain. The exercises below are designed to help you release tight muscles and strengthen weak ones, addressing the root causes of an anterior pelvic tilt. For optimal results, perform three sets of each exercise and aim to do them three to four times a week. When you feel less chronic pain, you can then move on to strength training, which we will cover in Chapter 9.

Taking the time to do corrective exercises may not be as exciting as high-intensity workouts, running, or sports, but embrace the process. With each movement, you're getting one step closer to healing chronic muscular pain.

Releasing Tight Muscles

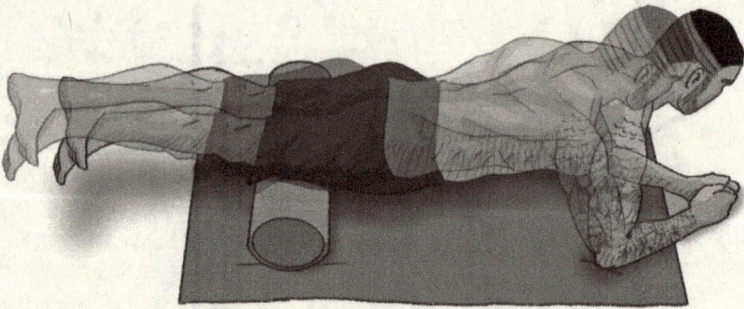

Quads and Hips: Use a foam roller to gently roll out your quadriceps for about 30 to 60 seconds on each leg. Then, transition the foam roller to target your hip area, spending another 30 to 60 seconds on each side. Rolling out these areas releases tension that accumulates across these interconnected muscle groups. Remember to breathe deeply while rolling to facilitate both muscle and emotional release.

Feet: Use a tennis ball to roll out any tension in your feet for about 30 seconds on each foot. As you progress, you can switch to a lacrosse ball for a more intensive release, again aiming for 30 seconds per foot.

Calves: Using a foam roller, apply gentle pressure to your calf muscle, moving from the ankle up to just below the knee. Spend approximately 30 to 60 seconds on each calf.

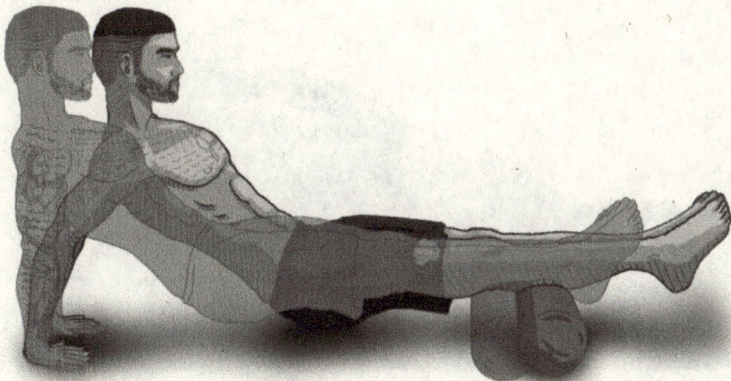

Strengthening Weak Muscles

Glute Clams: Lie on your side with your legs stacked and bent at a 90-degree angle. Rest your head on your lower arm, and either place your upper arm in front of you or brace it on your hip for balance, whichever feels more comfortable. Keeping your feet together, lift your top knee, calf, ankle, and foot to activate the glutes. This resembles a clam opening its shell. Pause at the top, then slowly lower and repeat. Complete three sets of twelve repetitions on each side.

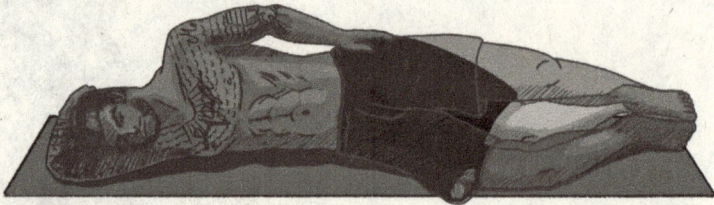

Glute Bridges: While lying on your back with knees bent, push upward through your heels, raising your hips as high as you can off the floor. Pause at the top, lower your hips back down in a controlled motion, and repeat. Complete three sets of twelve repetitions.

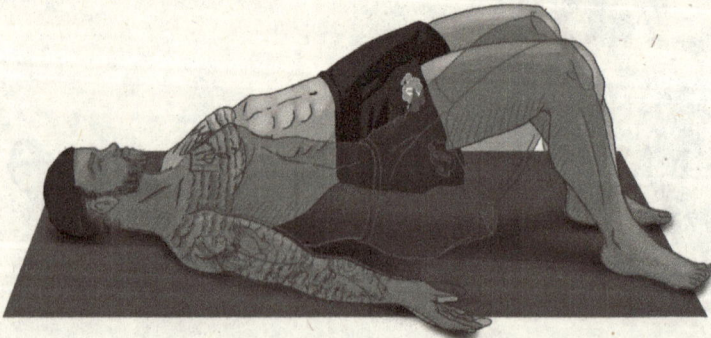

Leg Extensions: Lie on the ground with your palms facing up. With your back flat against the floor, raise your feet and bend your knees to a 90-degree angle. Alternate extending each leg one at a time, ensuring your back remains grounded. Start by performing this exercise for 30 seconds. Once this duration becomes comfortable and easy, advance to 45 seconds and then to a full minute as you progress. Aim for three sets of this duration-based exercise.

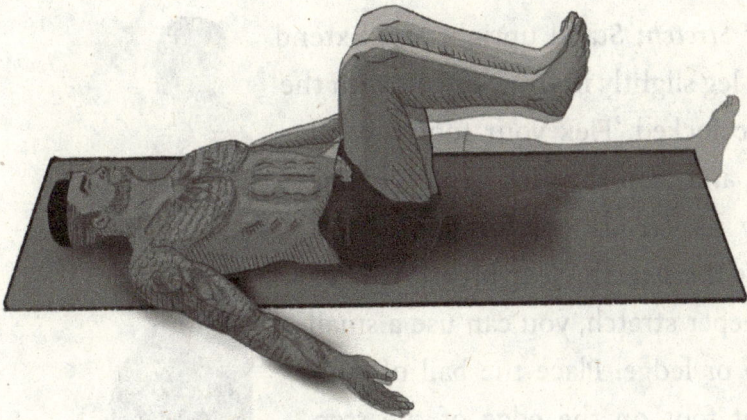

Stretching

Hip Flexor Stretch: Start by kneeling on the ground, placing one knee on the floor while the other foot is in front, forming a 90-degree angle with your knee. Ensure your torso is upright and engage the glute on the side with the knee on the ground. This engagement encourages your pel-vis to shift into a

posterior pelvic tilt, deepening the stretch. Gently push your hips forward until you feel a stretch in the front of your hip. Keep your torso upright and avoid arching your back. Hold this position and breathe deeply for 90 seconds. Repeat on the other side. For a deeper stretch, you can raise your arm on the same side as the kneeling leg and gently lean to the opposite side. Aim for three sets of 90 seconds for each side.

Calf Stretch: Stand upright and extend one leg slightly in front of you with the knee locked. Flex your foot toward you and lean forward gently, going only as far as comfortable—don't force the stretch. Keep breathing. For a deeper stretch, you can use a small step or ledge. Place the ball of your front foot on the edge of the step, keeping your heel on the ground. Lean forward gently, ensuring the stretch remains comfortable. Keep breathing. Aim for three sets of 90 seconds for each side.

Chest Release on Yoga Ball: Position your upper back onto a sturdy inflatable exercise ball. Extend your arms to open up your chest muscles. Practice deep breathing to facilitate the stretch. Hold this position, focusing on deep, relaxed breaths, until you feel a sense of calmness and relief in your chest and shoulders. There is no set duration for this stretch; hold it as long as it feels beneficial.

HEALING BY CHANGING SUBCONSCIOUS PATTERNS

This scenario might feel familiar: you start the new year with goals like eating better to heal digestion and exercising more to lose weight. You immediately shop for food to meal prep and get a gym membership. Then, three months pass, and you find yourself with the same issues you had before the new year. You wonder: *Why can't I change? What is wrong with me?*

The reason isn't that you're not capable of change or didn't put in enough effort; it's that you're stuck repeating automatic behavioral patterns. These automatic behaviors are rooted in the subconscious mind. Every moment of every day, the subconscious mind shapes how you make decisions in all areas of life, including your health. And the subconscious mind loves to keep you in your comfort zone, especially after trauma.

As you may remember from Chapter 2, neuropathways become altered after trauma, making you view every new situation through a trauma-influenced lens, constantly alert to threat or challenge. When your subconscious mind is focused on survival, it resists change and favors the safety and security of familiar patterns. New behaviors can feel uncertain or risky to the subconscious, and this can lead you to fall short with new health goals.

Fortunately, you can create new patterns—new habits—that will help you achieve your health goals by repeatedly engaging in specific actions or thoughts until they become automatic. However, you can only do this if you take consistent action with your healing practices. To achieve health and happiness, you must be an active *daily* participant in your own healing.

The biggest mistake most of my clients make is trying to do "too much" with things like supplements, working out, and meditation, which adds additional stress to their minds and bodies rather than healing them. They have an "all or nothing" mindset that often leaves them falling short of their goals. Why? Because the subconscious drive to fight or flight to survive makes them speed through life. Accomplishing goals is a process that requires patience and consistency. You can't eat better, heal your digestion, fix chronic muscular pain, or become the You You Never Knew until you become *aware* of this tendency to rush through the process and the need to embrace a more measured and mindful approach.

The thought *I can't afford to take my time* was deeply embedded in my subconscious because, at one point in my life, it was true. I had to actively seek safety and security on a daily basis. I didn't have the time to build long-term friendships, stay after school for tutoring, or allow myself a full night of rest. I had to find solutions to the problems I faced every day, such as helping my father make money for us to eat and sleep. Participating in friendships and school activities and pausing to rest all felt like threats to my survival.

As I progressed on my healing journey and moved beyond the need to focus on survival that marked my younger years, I too struggled with consistency in my health goals. I knew what I was supposed to do, but I wasn't doing it. Why? I was subconsciously rushing through my healing process as if I was still facing the daily challenges of making money for food and shelter. Even though I was now in a safe and secure environment, I was still stuck in old patterns. This is when I understood the crucial role the subconscious mind plays when trying to heal from trauma. It would be almost impossible to heal without incorporating changing subconscious patterns into my healing practices. I needed to first become more conscious of and deliberate and mindful about the healing process, instead of reacting on autopilot. Once I did, I was able to develop new habits to achieve my health goals.

As we work on healing from trauma, we need to be mindful—*conscious*—of the importance of making time for ourselves to do the work of changing our subconscious patterns. To heal, you need to allow enough time to rest; to be mindful of your nutrition and chew your food thoroughly; and to apply the corrective exercise program to overcome chronic muscular pain. Until you become more conscious that healing is a process that requires energy and time, you won't achieve your health goals. In other words, you can't succeed in healing while remaining in survival mode.

At first, this may feel foreign to you. Whenever we attempt to push ourselves out of our comfort zone, we face resistance from our mind and body. We'll talk more about resistance and how to overcome it in Chapter 8. In this case, this resistance will appear anytime you attempt to make time for yourself to heal; you may feel as if you are jeopardizing your survival. It might manifest in thoughts like, *Maybe I should check my email for work*, or *Let me see if a loved one needs me; I'll just check my phone, just in case*, or *Surely, there's something more productive I could be doing right now.* You may feel guilty, as if you are doing something wrong by deciding to take time for yourself to heal.

Feelings of responsibility and obligation can lead us to believe that everything and everyone else should be prioritized over our own needs, but this perspective is incorrect and draining. Before giving our energy and time to others, we need to rejuvenate ourselves. We can defeat feelings of guilt stemming from the subconscious mind by using the principle taught by my mentor Paul Chek: "I before We, and We before All." Start by taking care of "I"—that is, you. Only then can you move on to "We," which includes family and friends. Finally, you can look after "All," which includes work and anything outside your personal circle.[16]

Healing from trauma and rewiring the five layers of energy is a journey, not a quick fix. Consistency is the key to achieving any goal, but especially healing from trauma. To create lasting change, you need to take the necessary time to apply the healing practices discussed in this chapter and throughout this entire book. The more you become aware of old habits that create false perceptions and consciously make time for yourself to heal, the more consistent you will become.

To fully embrace this new way of living and receive its benefits, however, you need a compelling reason, a genuine desire, and a clear vision of a happier, healthier life—a strong enough *why* to motivate you to transform and make this new way of living subconscious. We will explore this topic in the next chapter.

6

THE YOU YOU NEVER KNEW

The You You Never Knew is a version of yourself that you aspire to be but have either failed to envision, due to a traumatic past, or not yet achieved because you were unaware of your sensitive nervous system. Trauma can leave your thoughts clouded by fear, and an unchecked sensitive nervous system results in a body overwhelmed by stress hormones. In that state, it's easy to feel numb and disconnected from inspiration. Emotions skew toward sadness, anger, powerlessness, and overwhelm. The body is primed for fight or flight, or it gets trapped in a "freeze" mode, impacting both physical and emotional well-being. In this hypervigilant state, where the body and mind are solely focused on managing and responding to immediate threats, there is little energy left to imagine or pursue any version of a better self. The constant need to stay safe makes it hard to see or strive for future goals, blocking any steps toward personal growth or change.

Transformation requires energy. Building that energy begins with taking control of what you can—your internal stressors—to consistently manage your sensitive nervous system. You began improving your energy by tackling the Trifecta Effect in Chapter 4. By preventing the blood sugar fluctuations that can trigger stress hormones like adrenaline and cortisol, you do more than just prevent stress—you also avoid fatigue. Now, with a solid foundation of stable energy, you're ready for the next vital step in taking control of your internal stress: *mastering your mindset.*

Trauma can alter your beliefs about yourself and others. It can create false perceptions about your worth and about the judgment of others that lead to feelings of insignificance. Together, these can shape your thoughts in ways that interfere with healing. By shifting the way you think, you start to rewire your self-perspective and beliefs. Positive thinking also significantly curbs the production of stress hormones by releasing feel-*good* chemicals like serotonin and dopamine, which help balance your mood, further breaking the Trifecta Effect. When it comes to healing from trauma, the power of changing your thoughts, self-perspective, and beliefs is profound. By taking control of your internal stressors, you'll be empowered to effect changes that influence your environment—your external stressors. We will explore this in more detail in the following chapters.

Creating the You You Never Knew doesn't begin at the end of the book; it starts now, in your mind. Because without the intrinsic motivation to change, it's hard to commit to any goal. Focusing on the new you acts as kryptonite to the negative thoughts, emotions, and self-perspective that your past has programmed into your sub-conscious. Deciding who you want to become and keeping that mental image in your mind is essential; without this, you will rely solely on willpower, and willpower, though powerful, is finite. It is rapidly depleted by stress, leaving us struggling with past thoughts, feelings, and behaviors. This is why relying solely on willpower to overcome trauma and stress falls short.

To succeed in fully becoming the You You Never Knew, you have to face another challenge—the subconscious mind.

HIDDEN POWER

The subconscious mind is a repository for our beliefs, values, habits, and traumas. Remarkably adept at multitasking, it seamlessly auto-mates essential functions such as breathing, digestion, blinking, and cell repair—tasks we carry out without a moment's thought. Every day, our subconscious quietly influences our choices, actions, and reactions. It's a hidden force shaping how we interact with the world, often without us realizing it.

The subconscious mind operates differently from the conscious mind. The conscious mind is where our "knowing" resides—it's the home of the thoughts and concerns we are actively aware of each day. The subconscious mind is our "doing" engine; it holds everything we've learned over time and subtly influences what we "know" and the actions we take based on that knowledge.

This explains why, despite knowing what we *should* do, we often fail to act . . . unless we make an action habitual—subconscious. As highlighted in Chapter 2, behavior becomes ingrained in our subconscious in two ways: through trauma or through repetition. We have minimal control over how trauma affects our subconscious. But through repetition, we have the ability to reprogram—rewire— our subconscious mind.

We've all purposefully made something subconscious before. Consider the skills you've mastered over years of practice, like driving or playing an instrument or even brushing your teeth. Through repetition, these skills became second nature, or subconscious, to the point where you no longer need to think about how to perform them. You just do. This is the same route you need to take to consistently manage your sensitive nervous system by taking control of your internal stressors.

As you aspire to become the You You Never Knew—happy, healthy, and inspired—you must become aware of the hidden power of your subconscious mind. Old beliefs, thoughts, and perspectives that no longer serve you can hinder your transformation. You can't change events that have already transpired, but you can choose how you respond to them. By deciding to control your narrative instead of allowing it to control you, you take a crucial step toward transformation.

PURSUIT OF PURPOSE

When we experience trauma or events that are beyond our control, we sometimes adopt a victim mindset. This isn't to say that those who've experienced trauma aren't victims in a real sense; they very much are. The problem is that that feeling of being a victim can embed itself into our subconscious. Eventually, it becomes part of our self-image—a mental representation of ourselves that influences our perceptions, attributes, abilities, and potential.

Perceiving yourself as a victim can make you believe you don't have the power to change your life. It makes you think you have to wait and hope for someone or something to rescue you from your pain and struggles. It's natural to want help—to wish for someone to see your suffering and lend a helping hand. However, if that help doesn't come, you can feel hopeless and lost, doubting your own ability to change your circumstances. This mindset makes it harder to manage your internal stress because it shifts your focus toward negative thoughts.

Negative thoughts trigger stress hormones, thus activating the Trifecta Effect. With this heightened stress, your focus shifts away from building a brighter future. Instead, you find yourself subconsciously reverting to survival mode, primarily concerned with the present moment and any immediate threats to your safety and security. Whenever you trigger the Trifecta Effect—whether by neglecting the nutritional strategies outlined in Chapter 4 or failing to change your thoughts, perspectives, and beliefs—you make managing your internal stressors that much harder.

When you change your perception of *you*, your entire world shifts. Suddenly, what you once saw as obstacles begin to appear as opportunities. Challenges that seemed impossible transform into stepping stones toward growth and success. Others' opinions and external circumstances lose their grip on your self-worth as you start to derive confidence from within. This shift brings clarity to your values and priorities, and your actions become more aligned with your true self. The world around you hasn't changed; your perspective has just unlocked a different way to experience and navigate it.

The first step in transforming your self-perception is detaching from the past. When you dwell on past experiences that negatively impacted your self-image, you're not just remembering them—you're reviving the emotions and thoughts, such as shame and guilt, associated with them. These emotions can stall your progress by triggering subconscious behaviors and reactions, reactivating old patterns that work against your healing. Instead of moving forward, you become stuck in a loop of past habits that reinforce the pain and prevent growth. It's as if the past casts a long shadow over your present, keeping you tied to the same place, unable to heal and step into a brighter future. To detach from the past, you have to make a decision about who you want to become and what you want in your life. You have to commit to the *Pursuit of Purpose.*

Just as you needed a reason to practice those other skills you've made subconscious over the years (the desire to get places yourself, to learn to play music, to maintain dental health), you need a strong reason to remain devoted to your transformational plan. You need a reason to consistently manage your sensitive nervous system. You need a purpose—a deep, intrinsic motivation and compass that guides you through life's challenges, including healing from trauma. It supports your present efforts to break the Trifecta Effect, aligns with your future aspirations, and unveils the You You Never Knew.

Your purpose could be to rediscover a passion you've put aside, to honor a loved one, or to contribute to a cause greater than yourself. Perhaps it's the desire to form healthier relationships, pursue a dream or career, regain control over your life, or simply to experience joy and satisfaction in daily activities. It might involve setting an example for your children, breaking generational cycles of trauma, or living true to your core values.

Your purpose serves as a means to regain control over your life. It helps you focus on a goal or aspiration beyond the subconscious reactions triggered by past traumas. More than just a source of motivation, your purpose is vital for healing. It's the *why* for managing your sensitive nervous system. Without it, your actions will feel pointless, and you'll lose your sense of direction and momentum on the path to healing. Purpose fills your journey with meaning and turns each step into a broader story of recovery and empowerment.

Trust me on this: I've seen the Pursuit of Purpose radically transform my clients' lives. Sadly, I've also observed what happens when someone isn't clear on their purpose or doesn't fully embrace it: it can make transformation impossible.

My mother has struggled with addiction for her entire life, and growing up, I always wondered why. She was part of an addiction rehab program that supported her with a community and appropriate medication, but she still couldn't change. She would stay clean for a month or so, then relapse. When she *was* clean, she would overindulge in junk food and watch TV all day. She had no clear plan, calling, or purpose for her life. This lack of purpose not only contributed to her relapse but also led her to compensate for her unhappiness with other addictive activities.

Then, when I was about eight years old, my older sister had a baby—and I saw a different mother. Suddenly, she was motivated to stay clean, which gave her the energy to resist subconscious patterns and help my sister raise her child. It was the first time in my life that things seemed normal. Over the next three years, my sister had two more babies, and we all took turns taking care of them. My mother was the best grandmother she could be.

It's clear to me now that my mother had found her *why*. She had Pursuit of Purpose. Being a grandmother gave her a compelling reason to change and transform herself, offering her a second chance at parenthood. She had learned invaluable lessons from her past experiences raising my siblings and me. Now, as a grandmother, she applied this wisdom, "the new her," to her interactions with her grandchildren.

Grandparenting gave her a purpose strong enough to fuel her transformation. It wasn't just about becoming someone new. It was about making amends and doing things differently and better this time around.

Unfortunately, it didn't last. In an incredibly heartbreaking and tragic turn of events, my young niece passed away and my sister and her boyfriend faced murder charges.

Given my mother's troubled criminal history, she was unable to secure custody of my nephews. The state of New Jersey intervened, and my nephews were removed from our family. This was the day my mother lost sight of her Pursuit of Purpose. She didn't just relapse. She escalated to more dangerous drugs that further aggravated her mental health issues. Within a week, I lost my family. I was eleven years old.

Where my mother's Pursuit of Purpose dimmed in the face of this tragedy, mine was born. I discovered as a teenager that my desire to change my family's paradigm empowered me to remain consistent with my goals. It served as my *why* to stay positive during difficult times. As a teenager, I had little to no control over my external stressors, but I did have control over how I reacted to them by managing my thoughts. This helped me resist fear and doubt, control my reactions, and become the hero of my own narrative.

Your Pursuit of Purpose is your *why*—the driving force that keeps you dedicated to managing your sensitive nervous system. This dedication leads to repetition, creating the pattern required to rewire the first layer of your energy—your nervous system. Easy, right? Not really. Your subconscious mind, shaped by past trauma and stress, instinctively responds to new ideas and goals with resistance. It challenges you with beliefs and thoughts born from your past, in an effort to keep you from your Pursuit of Purpose.

"AM I GOOD ENOUGH?"

If, while reading the last section, a possible purpose emerged in your consciousness, did the thought *Am I good enough?* also arise? If it did, I've got you covered, and if it didn't, you'll be prepared when it does.

Thoughts like *Am I good/smart/strong/rich enough for this?* automatically surface when you consider a new goal. When you consciously contemplate something that conflicts with your subconscious beliefs, the subconscious mind automatically responds with the reasons why you can't achieve it or why you're not good enough to do it in an effort to uphold past beliefs. This is your subconscious mind providing you with perceptions and feelings rooted in trauma or chronic stress. And it doesn't stop just because you are working toward positive change.

Think of your subconscious mind as representing the old version of yourself, while your new conscious thoughts of pursuing your purpose represent the new version. The "old you," shaped by trauma and chronic stress, operates from a desire for safety and security. Its intention is to protect you. However, as you grow and evolve, many of these protective measures become less necessary. And even though it's time for you to move on, the old you doesn't want to be left behind. It is wired into your neural pathways and resistant to change—even positive change.

The old you stops you from your Pursuit of Purpose by generating thoughts that instill fear. We can label these thoughts as *negative thoughts*—ones that create doubt and anxiety and steal your potential for creating joy in your life. The more you focus on these negative thoughts, the more you generate negative feelings, which reinforce the neural pathways that feed and sustain the old version of yourself. The key to retraining your thoughts and overcoming your old subconscious patterns is becoming aware that everything has polarity, or an opposite side.

Think of a coin. Every coin has two sides: heads and tails. The closer we look at one side of a coin, the more we lose sight of the coin's opposite side. Similarly, when we focus on negative thoughts, it diminishes our ability to recognize the opposite side of that negative thought—a positive one. For example, if you find yourself questioning, *Am I good enough?* flip that thought and remind yourself of all the reasons why you are more than good enough. I call this the *Coin Flip Method*.

The old you overlooks your past great achievements and the goodness that exists in your life today. By recognizing that there's another side to your doubts, you can flip negative thoughts into positive thoughts and, through repetition, retrain your subconscious mind to see your future potential. You unlock the ability to create feelings of inspiration and motivation. This feeds the "new you" and empowers you to pursue your purpose.

During the time my family and I lived in a motel in front of the Holland Tunnel, I found a way to remain grateful for the things I did have, even amidst all the trauma and stress I was enduring. Yes, I was homeless, and abused and abandoned by my mother, but I also lived across the river from one of the best cities in the world, New York City. I had a beautiful, upfront view of the New York City skyline, and I knew there were people in the world who wished they could wake up to that view every morning. This perspective shifted my focus from negative thoughts about my current circumstances to my hopes for my future. I realized that if I continued to stay positive in my thoughts, being so close to New York City would give me the opportunity to make a living there—which I eventually did. My first job and business were in New York City.

Whenever the old you brings up negative thoughts, flip the coin and reflect on all the great things you've accomplished in your life. Focus on everything you are grateful for. This shifts your perspective and changes your mental attitude.

Negative thoughts affect everyone, even those we perceive as better, smarter, stronger, or richer than we are. I have worked with professional athletes, Hollywood actors, and even multimillionaires—all of whom struggle with negative thoughts. However, those who overcome adversity in their lives have subconsciously developed a positive mental attitude. They automatically find the silver lining in every challenge and flip negative thoughts into positive ones.

Sometimes, we all need a reminder of our own power. This was something I learned from my client Hector Caraballo, an emergency room doctor who was transitioning to starting his own health and wellness business online. I noticed Dr. C's lack of confidence in his body language and the negative responses he gave whenever we discussed his Pursuit of Purpose: guiding people to health and happiness through his own blogs and podcasts. One day, I addressed it directly. "What's making you hesitant about your Pursuit of Purpose?" I asked. He took a deep breath and confessed, "I don't think I am smart enough to make this happen."

Due to Dr. C's unmanaged sensitive nervous system, he couldn't perceive the positive aspects of his situation, such as having more time to spend with his family and increased fulfillment from being able to globally reach and help people. He didn't have the mental energy to remind himself of his significant accomplishments: overcoming trauma and poverty and becoming a doctor. This is precisely why the first steps in my coaching program are to educate my clients about what a sensitive nervous system is and to provide a nutritional approach for healing. Then, we can embark on the Pursuit of Purpose. Without this foundational step—without breaking the Trifecta Effect—they struggle to control their thoughts, feelings, and perceptions. This activates their sensitive nervous system, leaving them overwhelmed by their goals and the energy they demand. Their goals appear too challenging to achieve.

After assisting Dr. C with his nutrition, it was time for the Coin Flip Method. I asked him, "Dr. C, how difficult was it to become a doctor, and how long did it take you?"

"Oh, wow," he answered. "It was very challenging. I didn't have anyone close to my family to guide me, and I had to figure it out on my own. Because of that, I went through years of trial and error, but eventually, I made it into medical school and then became a doctor. It took years."

"What thoughts dominated your journey then, positive or negative ones?" I asked.

"They were definitely positive. If they weren't, I wouldn't have made it," he answered, smiling as he began to see the direction of our conversation.

Dr. C embarked on his Pursuit of Purpose and realized his dreams by starting his own business. That Pursuit of Purpose became the motivation he needed to adhere to his nutritional plan. He now uses the Coin Flip Method whenever he sets goals that are bigger than his previous ones, to overcome the negative thoughts that accompany them.

Positive thoughts, reinforced through repetition and the Coin Flip Method, train the mind just like physical exercise strengthens the muscular system. The more you train, the stronger your mental resilience becomes. Over time, you subconsciously cultivate a positive mental attitude that enables you to see the good in every situation, maintain hope during difficult times, and believe in your ability to achieve your purpose.

This positive mindset serves as the key that unlocks opportunities, possibilities, and potential. A positive mindset doesn't require that you ignore the negative situations you encounter in life or pretend they don't exist. Instead, it means choosing to focus on the positive aspects, the potential, and the lessons to be learned, even in the face of adversity.

Living with an unmanaged sensitive nervous system makes positive thoughts more challenging. The effects of trauma and chronic stress on your subconscious obscure your awareness of the internal power you are born with, power that can propel you from where you are today to who you want to become tomorrow: the You You Never Knew.

THE POWER OF YOUR IMAGINATION

As we get older, we forget what a powerful tool the imagination is. When we're kids, our imaginations are wild and free from the limitations that "real life" places on us. We dream of being superheroes, astronauts, or professional athletes, and in our minds, those dreams are as real as anything. But as we grow older, many of us lose touch with this part of ourselves.

External influences—the people, environments, and traumatic events of our past—play a significant role in shaping our self-image. The feedback we receive from others, whether praise, criticism, or indifference, and the social standards and expectations we're exposed to through media and cultural norms, all contribute to how we perceive ourselves.

Fortunately, you have the power to alter your self-image—by using your imagination to craft a mental picture of a "new you."

I learned the power of a positive self-image from my elementary school counselor, Mr. Fernandez. He introduced me to the transformative practice of visualizing success. Every morning he would hand me clippings featuring athletes who had earned scholarships and encourage me to envision myself in their place. Eyes closed, I'd imagine my face on the page, my name in the headlines, celebrating these achievements as if they were already mine.

This daily ritual was a mental rehearsal for success and fostered a positive mindset that shielded me from the negative emotions and thoughts from challenges at home. Through regular visualization of an improved version of myself, I managed to regulate my emotions and sustain my optimism. Mr. Fernandez introduced me to the idea that self-image is a wellspring of empowerment. It was an invaluable lesson on the power of perspective—realizing that reshaping my self-perception could transform my emotional world and guide me along a constructive path. This wisdom from Mr. Fernandez is a gift I carry with me to this day, a technique I still employ to navigate life's journey.

Think about your Pursuit of Purpose. Imagine yourself achieving it. What does it look like? What does it feel like? How are you living? What kind of person are you? Take a moment to really visualize this in your mind. This is the power of your imagination at work. The more you immerse yourself in this image of the new you, the one who is living your purpose, the stronger your belief in its potential to become reality will grow.

Belief in your ability to become this new version of yourself is important because beliefs act as internal commands to the brain. Our beliefs subconsciously dictate how we perceive the world around us. If we believe we can heal from trauma, we see challenges as opportunities for growth. However, if we believe we cannot heal, these same challenges become insurmountable obstacles.

Embracing a belief in your Pursuit of Purpose fundamentally shifts this perspective, transforming thoughts from "I can't" to "I can." You feel hopeful and charged with enthusiasm, which translates into the will to act on your Pursuit of Purpose. By changing your *beliefs* to embrace positivity and possibility, you fuel *actions* that align with your goals, reshaping your life's journey. Without beliefs, you become disempowered.

The placebo effect is a perfect illustration of the profound connection between our beliefs and the physical responses in our bodies. In study after study, individuals have experienced real changes in their health after receiving treatments with no therapeutic value, simply because they believe they are receiving a genuine medical intervention. Their belief in the effectiveness of the placebo triggers a cascade of biochemical reactions in the brain, releasing endorphins and other neurotransmitters that can produce measurable physiological effects.

Integrating the power of imagination with the power of belief opens a fascinating gateway to shape your reality. Your subconscious mind can't tell the difference between what's happening right now and what you're picturing in your head. Ever wonder why dreams feel so real, complete with emotions and sensations? That's your brain treating your dreams as if they're actually real. When you envision yourself living your purpose, your brain begins to create new neural pathways that mirror this envisioned reality. It effectively rewires itself to adopt the belief that this is indeed who you are, and your brain and body act accordingly.

By focusing on your Pursuit of Purpose, shifting your thinking with the Coin Flip Method, and consistently visualizing the new you, your brain gradually rewires itself to subconsciously believe in this new identity. You get the chance to craft a self-image based on your own intentions rather than external pressures and expectations. And changing your self-image leads to a change in behavior—the kind of behavior necessary to break the Trifecta Effect and manage your sensitive nervous system.

YOUR PURSUIT OF PURPOSE

As you've seen, having a compelling reason for real change is essential for discovering the You You Never Knew. This requires having a goal or dream to pursue that gives you a sense of purpose.

The first writing prompt below will help you gain clarity on your purpose. The second prompt will assist you in reinforcing your purpose and embedding it into your subconscious.

Identifying Your Purpose

Take out your journal or a piece of paper, and spend some time with these questions:

1. What is one goal you've always had but never accomplished due to a lack of time, support, or belief that you could achieve it?
2. If you were to achieve that goal, how would it transform your life?
3. What are your top five goals for the year? Among these five, which goal, if accomplished right away, would have an immediate, transformative impact on your life?
4. What did you love to do when you were younger? What dreams did the younger you have?

Look for patterns or recurring themes in your responses. These patterns are clues to what drives you and what matters most in your life. Reflect on how these goals and dreams connect to the larger themes of purpose discussed in this chapter:

- Rediscovering a passion
- Honoring a loved one
- Contributing to a cause
- Forming healthier relationships
- Breaking generational cycles
- Living according to your true values

How do these aspirations align with your deepest motivations? Is there one powerful enough that it can help guide you through life's challenges? Think about which aspiration you are willing to pursue despite obstacles. That's your purpose.

Your Daily Purpose Contract

Now that we've identified your goal or purpose, it's essential that you take the next step—action. This practice is designed to retrain both your thoughts and perceptions to change your mindset and rewire your subconscious mind.

Start each day by writing down your purpose using the template on page 98. Do this for thirty consecutive days. By consistently affirming your purpose, you're actively altering your neural pathways to align your self-image with your ambitions.

The subconscious can even make something as simple as writing down your purpose every day a challenge, based on old habits and paradigms. If you forget to write your dream down one day, start over from Day One the following day. This isn't a punishment; it's part of the process of rewiring your mind, thoughts, and perceptions.

When you successfully complete this thirty-day commitment, take a moment to reflect on how this consistent practice has influenced your perspective. Ask yourself: Have your thoughts become more positive? Have you felt a shift in how you view challenges and opportunities? This reflection is crucial, as it helps confirm the deep integration of your purpose into your subconscious. If you notice that your perspective has positively evolved, you have successfully met the challenge. While you can choose to continue reinforcing these changes by writing down your purpose daily, it is no longer a requirement.

If you don't complete the thirty days successfully on your first attempt, don't be discouraged. Simply restart the process. Keep writing your purpose each day until it becomes second nature.

After writing your purpose each day, also jot down three things you're grateful for. These can be as simple or profound as you wish, and they can vary or remain the same from day to day. Incorporating this into your routine rewires your perceptions, helping to break the cycle of negative thoughts and emotions rooted in past traumas. By focusing on gratitude, you shift attention away from past pains and toward current blessings, which supports healing and helps you transform into the new you.

Your Purpose Contract

Purpose Statement

Write down your purpose in the form of an "I Am" statement. This should reflect your Pursuit of Purpose and can evolve over the thirty days as you gain more clarity.

Examples:

- "I am a creator who brings joy and insight to others through my art."
- "I am a compassionate practitioner committed to enhancing the well-being and health of those I serve."
- "I am an advocate for change, using my voice and actions to promote environmental sustainability and awareness."
- "I am a lifelong learner committed to expanding my knowledge and applying it to innovate within the tech industry."
- "I am a community leader who inspires and supports others to achieve their goals and strengthen our neighborhood."
- "I am a caring parent who nurtures my children's growth and happiness by providing love, guidance, and support."

Gratitude List

List three things you're grateful for. These can be as simple or as profound as you like and can change or stay the same day to day.

Example:

1. I am grateful for the support of my friends and family.

2. I am grateful for my health and the motivation to improve it each day.
3. I am grateful for the quiet moments in the morning that set the tone for my day.

Commitment

Each day for the next thirty days, I commit to writing down my purpose and my gratitude list in my journal. I will sign this entry daily, treating it as if it were a contract. This practice will create a positive mindset and also rewire my brain to recognize the good in my life, even amidst challenges.

Signature and Date:

_____   _____

[Your Signature]   [Date of Commitment]

FROM VICTIM TO HERO

By embracing our power to transform our thoughts and perspectives, and by deciding to control our narrative instead of being ruled by those of others, we reclaim our strength. We move from a victim mindset to a hero mindset.

A hero is someone who overcomes challenges—who moves from a state of powerlessness to embrace personal empowerment and responsibility. Heroes embody resilience and courage in the face of challenges. They don't shy away from adversity, but face it head-on, drawing lessons and strength from their past experiences.

When you decide what you want and who you wish to become, and define your purpose, you stop letting life just happen. You begin becoming the You You Never Knew.

7

PROTECTING YOUR ENERGY

In Chapter 4, I wrote about how my brother, father, and I lived in a motel room, which my father paid for by selling his prescribed pain medication. As he aged, his disability, which seriously affected his hips, became more severe and limited his ability to walk. So, as the eldest son, I had to occasionally step in and become the drug runner. In the beginning, I was very naive and didn't understand what I was doing. But even once I did, I had to do what was necessary for us to survive.

My father would hand me a rolled-up brown paper bag with instructions about who to find and how much money to expect. I had to count the cash and make sure I received the full amount before the buyer could leave. As I grew older and got my license, I drove to meet the buyers instead of them coming to us. This added a new layer of stress and anxiety to my role, and I felt guilty every time I did a "run." The average run usually took about forty-five minutes, and I was hypervigilant the entire time. I was always looking for the police and praying they didn't stop me.

My childhood was already full of traumatic police encounters. They kicked down our door at least once a year, and I witnessed my loved ones being taken away. My family members weren't bad people in my eyes. They were survivors navigating their own traumas and striving to make a living. And their arrests often fell into two categories: for being under the influence, and for selling drugs. I saw both sides and empathized with both.

Growing up, my father had a warrant out for his arrest, which meant that evading the police was a routine part of my daily life. I learned to perceive the world around me as a threat, particularly the police. Just seeing a police officer would send my heart rate soaring. My body became hot, and my breathing turned rapid and shallow. I felt disconnected from my physical self. Despite my innocence, my thoughts were dominated by the fear of going to jail.

All of this made sticking to my nutritional goals—which were crucial for maintaining my energy levels, focusing in school, and managing my mood—difficult. Stress would trigger a return to old habits, especially overeating, a coping mechanism rooted in my childhood. Yet, amidst all the chaos, I somehow found the strength to achieve my goals. I received my full basketball scholarship to St. Anthony High School. However, I knew that one misstep could jeopardize everything. I quickly became aware of how important it was to protect my energy.

I noticed a sense of disconnection from my mind, body, and emotions whenever I was with my childhood friends or in my old neighborhood, a place known for being unsafe. This disconnection mirrored the feelings I experienced whenever I encountered a police officer. Acknowledging this, I began to distance myself from those friends, many of whom were deeply involved in the street life, as well as from my old neighborhood.

My strategy was successful: I graduated high school and went on to college on a full football scholarship. However, my battles with the perceptions, sensations, thoughts, and feelings that stemmed from my trauma didn't end there. Upon arriving at college, I found myself unable to trust anyone, and I often chose isolation. This behavior was a subconscious reaction—one that made sense for the environment I'd grown up in but was an overreaction to my current circumstances. I wasn't initially aware of this until a counselor pointed it out, but once it was brought to my attention, I became curious about the root cause. This realization, which came during my college years, led me to understand how my trauma was influencing me and to recognize that I have a sensitive nervous system.

When I came home from college for winter break, my dad asked me to make a run for him, and, for the first time, I said no. I explained to my father how uncomfortable the runs made me feel. I told him about my bodily reactions—sweating, shaking, and breathing issues—and how I believed they were signs of trauma. Since starting college, I'd left "survival mode" behind, along with the people I knew who were struggling with it. I also became more aware of how unusual my upbringing and home life were.

When I shared my traumas with my father, he opened up and spoke with me for hours. In these heart-to-heart conversations, I saw a side of him I'd never seen before—a man who also carried his own fears and traumas. This was a profound revelation to me.

It became clear that my father had been doing everything he could to provide for us, even at the cost of selling his pain medication for survival. Most importantly, I realized my father had never had anyone he could express his trauma to, because trauma was normal where he came from. That was when I started to understand the importance of setting boundaries, standing up for myself, and *protecting my energy*.

Protecting your energy is the essential practice of separating yourself from environmental factors, people, and circumstances that deplete the energy necessary for managing your sensitive nervous system and pursuing your purpose. Although it's important for everyone to protect their energy, it is especially critical for those of us with sensitive nervous systems. For us, external stressors do more than just trigger the nervous system. They overstimulate it, kicking off the Trifecta Effect, which interferes with our ability to consistently manage internal stressors.

As we've seen, once trauma or chronic stress embeds itself in your subconscious, it significantly shapes your emotions, thoughts, perceptions, and internal sensations. The body's subconscious response to past trauma causes the sensitive nervous system to overreact, drawing on past experiences related to these stressors, which makes your responses to both external and internal disturbances more intense. Strategies like breaking the Trifecta Effect and finding your Pursuit of Purpose give you the power to transform your internal world, fostering inspiration, cultivating positive thoughts, and looking at yourself as a hero rather than a victim.

It's important, however, to recognize that some people, environments, and circumstances trigger stress more than others. They evoke feelings of fear or anxiety that lead to negative thoughts, which ultimately reinforce the old you. This not only drains your energy but also hinders your Pursuit of Purpose.

We have the power to protect our energy by making thoughtful choices about the people we spend time with, the environments we immerse ourselves in, and where we focus our attention. We can avoid letting ourselves be consumed by energy-draining distractions. While we can't control external stressors like natural disasters, economic fluctuations, politics, and shifts in the workplace, we can become more mindful of how to limit their impact. In today's world we are exposed to myriad disagreements within our society, amplified by the rapid spread of information via media at our fingertips.

Instead of spending time on social media, we can choose to engage with resources that support our goals and healing. For instance, engaging with resources such as books and learning materials that align with our goals can significantly support our personal growth. Over time, this practice can become a habit that helps us focus on our purpose and cultivates a positive, growth-oriented mindset. By intentionally shaping these areas of our lives, we build a shield around our well-being.

Of course, this is easier said than done. Despite being aware that certain people, environments, and distractions aren't beneficial for us, we often find ourselves gravitating toward them. This puzzling behavior can be attributed to a subconscious tendency commonly known as being a *people pleaser*.

THE PEOPLE PLEASER

A sensitive nervous system not only heightens our sensitivity to our own emotions; it also amplifies our empathy toward others. When we're surrounded by individuals who are needy, easily distracted, and entrenched in a victim mentality, our heightened emotional sensitivity and empathy can lead us to devote excessive time and energy to their needs. This, in turn, diverts our focus from our own needs and aspirations, making it challenging to pursue our personal goals and dreams.

Even when you genuinely wish to say no to requests, the fear of conflict and a desire for safety and stability can overwhelm your nervous system, making that "no" difficult to voice. As a result, you might constantly find yourself saying yes to fulfilling others' needs. Over time, it can feel like you're wearing a mask: a facade focused on pleasing others at the expense of your own happiness. The longer you wear this mask, the more difficult it becomes to remove it, and the more you risk losing connection with your authentic self.

It's crucial to understand that a sensitive nervous system isn't the primary reason for this pattern; rather, it's the fear of being alone. Saying no can trigger a fear of losing your connection with friends and family members. Past traumas might have led to trust issues, hesitancy about making new friends, and a pervasive fear of losing the people you love, especially if you've previously experienced significant losses. Traumatic events can plant the deep-seated subconscious belief that you don't deserve love and respect for being who you truly are. As a result, you may find yourself seeking approval and validation from those around you—even if they drain your energy.

Chronic stress can contribute to a sense of isolation by intensifying the feeling that you are different than the people around you. When you're working to become a new version of yourself, this stress-driven sense of isolation can be further aggravated by fears of losing your social network. This cycle reinforces existing stress and trauma and hinders your ability to form the meaningful connections that are vital for personal development and emotional well-being.

How do you say no without letting your deepest fears get in the way? By prioritizing yourself. Now that you have a vision for the life you want to build—the new you—you've gained clarity and direction. You've moved beyond the victim mindset and are taking steps toward your purpose. While the idea of losing those close to you is daunting, consider the impact of not pursuing healing. By dedicating yourself to your own healing journey, you not only transform your life but also become a source of strength and inspiration for others. The consequences of neglecting your healing journey are greater than the consequences of pursuing it.

The transformation of my client Olivia is a vivid illustration of the journey from being a people pleaser to someone who understands the importance of self-care and setting boundaries. Her low self-esteem, a by-product of years spent in the shadow of an abusive father and subsequent relationships with manipulative partners, had rendered her a stranger to her own needs and dreams. Her life was an endless cycle of attending to others at the expense of her well-being.

In our coaching sessions, Olivia's biggest challenge was breaking through the ingrained belief that her own aspirations should always come second. Her reluctance to prioritize herself was deep-seated, stemming from the way past experiences had shaped her subconscious, and manifested in muscle tension and digestive issues, clear indicators of the Trifecta Effect at work.

When I prompted Olivia to contemplate her dreams and aspirations, she was initially lost. It was a concept so foreign to her that it seemed almost indulgent. But as we peeled back the layers, her true desires began to surface. She yearned to own her own business, a dream obscured by years of placing others' needs before her own.

The breakthrough came when she recognized that her perpetual readiness to serve others at her own expense was not an obligation but a choice, and she could adjust the balance. By adding her needs into the equation, Olivia began to reclaim her life. With each training session, she not only shed the physical weight she was carrying but also the emotional baggage that had long held her back.

As Olivia's coach, my role extended beyond physical training; it was about guiding her to a place where she could appreciate her worth and potential. By establishing clear goals and a supportive environment, we transformed the doubt that had trapped her into a belief that uplifted her.

Olivia's success, not only in losing weight and improving her posture, but eventually in starting her business, was a testament to her newfound self-image. She no longer carried guilt for prioritizing her own needs and began to exude a positivity that was once foreign to her.

Reflect on the amount of time and energy you dedicate to people who don't give the same to you in return. Now, imagine redirecting that energy and time back into your own growth and healing. Would this redirection help or hurt your healing process and Pursuit of Purpose? Focusing on yourself doesn't mean you'll lose everyone around you. It means you might distance yourself from those who hold you back and who don't deserve your time and energy when you're able to offer it.

Because of your nervous system's susceptibility to energy depletion, taking the time to balance and nurture your mind, body, and emotions is essential. Through this process, you become increasingly aware of the need to protect your energy by setting boundaries. Boundaries serve as a shield—they aren't meant to push people away but to protect you from behaviors and situations that drain your energy.

BOUNDARIES

Strong boundaries are an important and healthy practice for maintaining personal well-being, especially when healing from trauma. A boundary is a guideline or limit that you set to help people around you understand how you want to be treated. It is not an attempt to control someone else's behavior or to impose demands. Rather, it is a way of protecting your mental, physical, and emotional health. These days the term is becoming overused, and some people invoke it as a way to avoid confronting their own issues or to sidestep difficult conversations, particularly in the realm of personal development. Used properly, however, boundaries are essential for managing a sensitive nervous system.

Our sensitivity makes it hard not to feel and react emotionally to external stressors. Boundaries are the invisible lines we draw around ourselves to delineate our personal limits and communicate to others what we will and will not tolerate. They empower us to protect our energy reserves and ensure we're not constantly overwhelmed or drained by the demands and dynamics of the outside world.

Clear boundaries define what is acceptable and what isn't in your interactions with the people around you. For example:

- Having scheduled daily time for activities like exercise and reading that cannot be interrupted
- Being selective about which parts of your life you are willing to share on social media
- Respecting diverse viewpoints and expecting the same courtesy in return
- Taking time alone to recharge when you feel overwhelmed
- Expecting others to maintain a respectful distance, especially in close settings

Setting boundaries is especially crucial in your own home. With all of life's demands, from unexpected family visits to nonstop work notifications, finding a quiet moment can feel like an elusive dream. Just as you're settling into some well-deserved downtime, interruptions come knocking (sometimes literally) and demand your attention.

The first step in establishing the boundaries you need to protect your energy is to figure out what makes you feel secure, balanced, and at peace. For example, decide on a specific time—say, 8 PM—to set your phone to *do not disturb* mode, and stick to it. Disconnect from the pressures of the day, and truly unwind. Let your evenings become your sanctuary, a time dedicated to meaningful interactions with loved ones or time for yourself. Establishing such boundaries is a powerful step toward maintaining your inner peace and creating a balanced life.

Remember, you are not doing this to dodge responsibilities. You are choosing to rest your sensitive nervous system over responding immediately to every alert that comes your way.

When it comes to family, setting clear expectations about when you're available—whether for conversations over the phone or activities at home—is key. Creating a mutual understanding with those you live with in particular ensures that everyone's needs for space and connection are met.

Creating boundaries regarding the environments you are willing to enter is also essential, especially in places filled with excessive noise, crowds, and distractions. While others might thrive in these lively environments, if you have a sensitive nervous system, it's easy to become overwhelmed. It's okay to decline invitations to events that feel too stressful or to plan brief, manageable visits in places that have a quiet space you can retreat to if needed. By doing this, you honor your needs while still engaging with the world at your own pace.

For a long time, I avoided my old neighborhood to prevent triggering my PTSD. I sometimes worried about missing out, but focusing on my personal growth taught me that the places I associate with pain can distract me. Instead of using my energy for growth and healing, I find my nervous system drained by worries of safety and security. That's something I didn't mind missing out on.

As you evolve into the new you, the boundaries you set serve as a shield. They guide you on when to say no, sparing you the stress of overthinking. Over time, they seamlessly integrate into the fabric of the new you and support your *core values*, the beliefs and guiding principles that shape your behavior and actions.

Your core values shape how you interact with others, the decisions you make, and how you view the world around you. They are deeply rooted in your identity and act as a compass that guides the direction of your life. They ensure that your actions are in harmony with your authentic self. At their essence, core values are what fuel and inspire you. They mold your character and influence how you lead your life. They also undergo changes to align with your growth and the new direction of your life.

Boundaries based on your core values don't just apply to your interactions with people. It's crucial to also extend them to your physical environments—particularly in relation to food. Setting specific dietary limits, such as excluding processed foods and ensuring that your home environment only includes foods that support your sensitive nervous system, establishes clear boundaries regarding your surroundings. These boundaries can be integral to your healing journey.

When you are striving to mitigate the impact of your sensitive nervous system by breaking the Trifecta Effect, the presence of certain foods can tempt you, requiring willpower (which you'll recall is a limited resource) to avoid. Ensuring that your environment, especially at home, only contains foods that support your health objectives is a form of establishing boundaries with your surroundings. This proactive approach reduces the need for constant self-control and reinforces your core values, making it easier to live by them.

Now, I must warn you about what comes next. Living as your new, authentic self can unsettle those around you who haven't embraced their own purpose. You might find that these individuals disrespect your boundaries or challenge your "no." Either immediately or over time, they may begin to criticize you—not from malice, but because your growth serves as a reminder that they, too, need to begin a journey of self-care and personal development. This constant negativity can drain your energy and distract you from your own goals. Continuing to prioritize these relationships can be destructive, pulling you away from the positive steps you're taking toward healing from trauma.

YOUR BOUNDARIES

Write down your list of boundaries, which should be based on your core values. Describe what is acceptable and what isn't in your interactions with people around you. Reflect on why each one is crucial to you. These boundaries should align with your purpose and protect both your energy and your time.

- What elements do you need to start your day right?
- What do you need to wind down in the evening? What is your ideal bedtime, and how might you protect it?
- What kinds of people bring you down and how can you limit your interactions with them?
- Are there places or environments that drain your energy or trigger the old you and unhealthy habits? How can you avoid them?

- Are there forms of entertainment that you enjoy but that also distract you from your purpose? How can you enjoy them in a balanced way?

DREAM TEAM TRYOUTS

*"Your 'yes' isn't good enough until you learn
to say no. When someone respects your no,
they become part of your dream team."*
— Paul Chek[17]

Once you've determined your boundaries, you have to decide who deserves your time and energy as you pursue the new you. It's time to employ what I like to call *dream team tryouts*—a method for reevaluating which of your relationships serve your well-being and which do not.

Your dream team consists of people who support your purpose in life and whose purpose you support in turn. These individuals are like-minded people who accept and celebrate the new you, who deserve your time, energy, and creative ideas when you have the capacity to share. They respect your boundaries and don't take them personally, and they contribute positive, rather than negative, energy. When your energy is low, they lift you up, not make you feel worse. They, too, are focusing on their Pursuit of Purpose, brimming with inspiration and information.

In contrast, those who don't respect your boundaries and core values don't make the cut. They're not part of your dream team because they bring fear, negativity, and judgment to your life. Their presence stimulates your sensitive nervous system, which undermines your healing process by keeping you locked in unhealthy defensive patterns.

Clearly communicating your boundaries and core values to those around you may feel overwhelming at first. Enforcing your boundaries with certain individuals can leave you feeling guilty, especially if they don't have others who invest time and energy in them. The mere thought of asserting yourself can send your sensitive nervous system into overdrive. It can be useful to practice the Coin Flip Method here and view the situation from another angle. Saying no to those who don't merit your time and energy is essentially saying yes to yourself and like-minded individuals. With this perspective, we can feel less guilty about saying no.

Tryouts for your dream team unfold like this: when a situation arises in which saying yes would violate your boundaries, pay attention to how people react when you decline. Those who respect your "no" and support your decision are awarded a dream team jersey. Those who challenge your boundaries or disregard your core values get cut.

These tryouts can be stressful. Saying no to my father when he wanted me to do another run for him felt overwhelming; I feared how he would react. However, when he respected my "no," it confirmed that he truly was an essential part of my dream team.

As you're reading this, you may be noticing that some individuals close to you do not qualify for your dream team. You might be realizing that your previous attempts to heal from trauma and stress were hindered by their presence. They made it challenging for you to evolve into the new you.

There were people I cared for deeply who didn't make the team. This didn't mean I cut them out of my life entirely (although some I did). It meant I became cautious about the time and energy I invested in them, and I held back from sharing my goals for the future with them.

In some cases, staying true to my core values meant separating myself from people I love. It's been around fifteen years since I last saw my older brother and sister. While they were using their energy to pursue crime, I was dedicated to pursuing change by overcoming generational trauma and poverty. As much as I care about them, I had to protect myself and my energy.

Yes, there were times when I was alone, but I soon learned how necessary solitude can be for healing. Protecting your energy is about more than simply avoiding negative influences; it's about freeing up time and space to embrace learning and personal growth. Education is essential for becoming the new you. You need to acquire new skills, develop the discipline to persevere, and allow time for trial and error. You need time to learn from your mistakes. Not to mention grocery shop and prepare meals to help you stay consistent with breaking the Trifecta Effect. You can't afford to have your time and energy depleted. The more you understand the importance of this time for transformation, the easier it is to prioritize your needs.

Now, you will discover that certain people respect your "no" occasionally but not consistently. I call these individuals "bench players." They may not show full support yet, but they have the potential to do so. As you continue on your Pursuit of Purpose, some of these bench players may gradually grow and improve to the point where they earn their place on the team, while others may never meet the mark. It's perfectly fine if some individuals need more time to align with your core values and consistently respect your boundaries. However, it's important to recognize patterns where your boundaries are repeatedly disregarded. This helps you determine when giving more chances may not be beneficial.

BUILDING YOUR TEAM ROSTER

It's time to identify who truly deserves a spot on your dream team.

Consider the top ten people you interact with regularly. This can be family, friends, coworkers, or others. For each person, ask yourself:

- Do they respect and support my core values?
- How do they react when I assert my boundaries or say no?
- Do they encourage my growth, or do they bring negativity?

Categorize these individuals into three groups, based on your reflections:

- **Dream team players:** Those who consistently respect your values and boundaries.
- **Bench players:** Those who sometimes support your values and show potential, but need a bit more time to grow.
- **Not on the team:** Those who regularly challenge or disregard your values and boundaries.

Reflect on your list.

- How does it feel to realize who truly supports you?
- Were there any surprises on your list?
- How can you adjust the way you use your time and energy to prioritize your dream team players?
- What strategies can you implement to manage your interactions with those who are not on your team?

＊

THE STOPWATCH METHOD

It's not always easy to avoid people who aren't on your dream team. Think about it: whether it's during holiday gatherings, at family get-togethers, or at work, there are times when you'll find yourself around people who just don't gel with your vibe. Honestly, just thinking about being around certain individuals used to stress me out so much that I'd lose sleep the night before. I'd get all worked up, knowing how much their comments, drama, and wild behavior always threw me off. That's when I came up with the *Stopwatch Method.*

The Stopwatch Method is about setting time limits. Whenever I head into a situation where I'll be around people who are not on my dream team, I decide beforehand how long I'm going to stick around. Then I set a timer on my watch, like a countdown. If someone starts gossiping, throwing shade, or acting a fool around me, I just check my watch and remind myself, *I'm out of here in an hour. If this is how they want to spend it, that's on them.* This mindset gives me the strength to handle these moments. I know there's an exit plan.

Ideally, we would avoid events and environments that trigger our nervous systems entirely, but that's not always possible. The Stopwatch Method offers a strategic approach for situations where we can't. It's a way of protecting our boundaries and core values in these contexts by introducing an additional boundary: a time limit. We are honoring the importance of our time, especially when we have to spend it expending extra energy just to sustain ourselves.

What's remarkable is that, when you adhere to these time limits, people begin to take notice. They come to understand that you are not interested in wasting your time on negativity. Over time, many start to adjust their behavior and adopt a more positive demeanor in your presence. Setting boundaries doesn't only benefit you. It also prompts others to reconsider their actions.

When you're headed into a situation with folks who are not on your dream team, decide how long you're willing to spend with them, and once that time's up, it's okay to leave. Don't feel guilty about it. Remember, setting boundaries is essential to protect your own well-being. If they start showing more positive vibes over time, then you can consider giving them a bit more of your time in the future.

USING THE STOPWATCH METHOD

Employ this method for any upcoming event where you might be around people who don't align with your energy.

Establish your boundaries.

- How long can you be around these individuals before you start to feel drained or negative?
- What behaviors and comments from others will alert you that it's time to leave an event to avoid feeling overwhelmed?

Set your time limit.

- How long will you plan to stay?
- How will you remind yourself about this time limit during the event?

Have an exit strategy.

- Imagine the event is underway. How will you handle situations or conversations that start to turn negative? (You can throw in a lighthearted comment or a funny joke, for example, to shift the vibe, or steer the conversation gently toward a neutral or positive topic.)
- Think about potential phrases or strategies to redirect the conversation or gracefully excuse yourself, such as excusing yourself to refresh your drink, greet anther guest, or check on something.

Reflect after the event.

- How did it go? Did setting a time limit help?

- Were there any noticeable changes in how people interacted with you?
- How did you feel when you left?

Think about next time.

- How can the Stopwatch Method be a tool for future interactions? Think about how this approach can empower you and potentially influence those around you.

THE ART OF PROTECTING YOUR ENERGY ON THE PATH TO TRANSFORMATION

Becoming the You You Never Knew is all about evolution, growth, and transformation. This path is like a garden where the seeds of your potential are planted. Like any garden, you need the right conditions to thrive. Your energy is the sunlight, water, and nutrients your garden needs. When you allow negative energies or influences to invade, it's like letting weeds overrun your garden.

By surrounding yourself with those who align with your purpose—your dream team—you're giving your garden the best chance to flourish. By setting boundaries, you're preventing weeds from taking root. By taking steps like the Stopwatch Method to ensure you stay in alignment with your boundaries and core values, you're nurturing the soil.

Remember, a new you is waiting just beneath the surface, ready to emerge in full bloom. But this transformation requires a harmonious environment, where your energy is valued, respected, and protected. As you move forward on this journey, reflect on the environments and people you surround yourself with. Ask yourself, *Are they nourishing my growth or hindering it?* By consciously curating your surroundings and interactions, you're not just protecting your energy but championing your evolution.

Sadly, you will soon discover that the greatest battle isn't with those around you but rather the one within yourself. It's vital to brace yourself for the inevitable resistance posed by the old you. This resistance prevents you from stepping out of your comfort zone by inundating your mind, body, and emotions with its closest tool—fear. In the next chapter, we will look at strategies to confront and overcome this internal resistance, turn inner battles into victories, and embrace fear as a catalyst for growth.

8

FROM FEAR TO COURAGE

Becoming the new you is a beautiful journey of transforma-
tion, one that inevitably guides you into uncharted territories of
change—into the unknown, where fear arises. And those of us with
a traumatic past can find ourselves haunted by three fears in particular: the fear of failure, the fear of rejection, and, surprisingly, the
fear of success.

The first of these fears stems from a subconscious association
of failure or mistakes with severe consequences, such as punishment from an authority figure or having to return to survival mode,
where concerns for safety and security dominate our daily lives.
The second fear, rejection, comes from putting ourselves out there,
perhaps for the first time, after years of not living our true purpose.
We worry that we won't be accepted when we do. Finally, there's

the fear of success, which arises from the uncertainty of how our lives might change once we achieve our goals. This fear can involve concerns about increased responsibilities, higher expectations, and the possibility of losing our current identity and relationships.

Regardless of the type of fear you struggle with, fear is still fear. What's more important is recognizing how fear manifests itself. Without this awareness, you may not realize when it's interfering with your Pursuit of Purpose, protection of your energy, or healing from trauma. And it's impossible to defeat an enemy you do not understand.

Fear presents itself as resistance. This resistance can manifest in various ways. It can feel like avoidance, steering clear of situations or activities that challenge you, or self-doubt, questioning your abilities and worth. It can also show up physically as tension, headaches, or fatigue, and emotionally as anxiety and irritability. This resistance is natural. It tells you that you are facing something meaningful that demands energy and attention. But for those with trauma, it can feel like overwhelming pressure. Instead of just making you feel hesitant or doubtful, even small tasks can seem insurmountable and paralyzing. It's as if any step forward is too much to bear.

This pressure, stemming from fear, almost always surfaces during any transformation as part of your old self's plan: trying to protect you from further stress and trauma. Remember, the old you is deeply embedded in your subconscious mind, influencing not just your thoughts and emotions but your nervous system. This is why it's so important to follow the steps for healing trauma and chronic stress provided in the previous chapters. If you aren't succeeding in breaking the Trifecta Effect, conquering resistance will be that much harder. Just as you began to rewire your thoughts with the Coin Flip Method in Chapter 6, you must now apply a similar approach to manage the sensations, feelings, and perceptions arising from the old you's resistance to change.

Let's revisit the coin analogy. Imagine one side of the coin represents the old you; the other side is the new you. The coin has been stuck to an object so that only the old you side shows. Over time, the coin has become fused with the object. When you try to remove the coin to reveal its other side, you encounter resistance. You tightly grip the edge of the coin, bite down on your lip in determination, and prepare to pull with all your might. You envision the other side and the potential for change. But you meet with resistance—the coin has become part of the object. And the longer it's been there, the tougher it is to detach.

The old you embodies your past, the new you symbolizes your future, and the edge of the coin represents the now—the middle ground, where transformation takes place. It's where potential and resistance coexist as you take action.

As you transition from the old version of yourself to the You You Never Knew, resistance is inevitable. If you don't confront your fears, you'll yield to the resistance that accompanies transformation and miss the chance to realize your potential for change. If you do confront your fears, and overcome this resistance, your perspectives shift. You start to see the beauty in resistance; you understand that it emerges whenever there's an opportunity for change.

PERFECTIONISM AND PROCRASTINATION

Whenever I coach a client who shows signs of perfectionism, I always look for its twin, which often accompanies it—procrastination. Both perfectionism and procrastination can be rooted in trauma and become habit through repetition. They are two of the primary forms of resistance to confront during the process of healing from trauma.

Perfectionism leads us to focus on our perceived flaws rather than recognizing our own beauty and gifts. It stems from the fear of failure and a need for acceptance. We dread the consequences that may follow failure, especially if we've faced harsh consequences or punishment for mistakes in the past. We fear losing the acceptance of others if we are not perfect.

This fear of being seen for who we are—imperfect—leads us to procrastinate. We start coming up with seemingly logical reasons to postpone our transformation efforts. We persuade ourselves that further research or preparation is necessary before we can proceed. We end up waiting for the "perfect" moment to take action—something that does not exist. Looking for the perfect moment ultimately delays or prevents us from achieving our transformation goals.

While procrastination can be a reaction to perfectionism, it can also stem from an underlying fear of success, where we hesitate to make changes that could fundamentally alter our lives. Even when we know our new life will be better, the truth is, change is scary. Change is challenging no matter what.

This fear can lead us to avoid taking the steps necessary for transformation, keeping us in a comfortable, familiar state that ultimately hinders our growth.

Perfectionism tells us, "If it can't be perfect, why bother starting?" Procrastination whispers, "Tomorrow is a better day to begin." Both perfectionism and procrastination lead to avoidance, which convinces us, "It's easier not to face this at all." These voices are persuasive, but they are also deceiving.

Avoiding action on our goals does not save us from failure and rejection. Instead, it leads us directly to it. A failure to make headway on our goals becomes yet another source of stress that triggers the Trifecta Effect. So, how do we react? With more avoidance. We shy away from even contemplating our health goals and purpose because the thought of them becomes too stressful. As the saying goes, *Striving for perfection is the first step to failure*.

So, what is the first step to conquering resistance? Courage.

LEADING WITH COURAGE

Just as resistance naturally arises from fear, so does courage. Within each of us lies the potential for courage—a powerful force, the *will*, to conquer resistance. Embracing this force means stepping up and taking responsibility for your actions and decisions despite the fear. Courage means facing challenges head-on, even when it seems easier to give up, and showing that you can rise above the past and its limitations.

Like resistance, courage can take many forms, making it hard to perfectly define. However, you recognize courage when you *feel* it. Courage requires commitment, perseverance, truth, and willingness to *answer the call*. All of these qualities are essential for healing from trauma.

The Courage to Commit

It takes courage to say, "I am not going to allow fear to stop me from healing." It takes courage to say, "I will be the one in my family who changes generational trauma and poverty." But there is no courage without commitment: setting clear goals and sticking to them, even when obstacles arise and the path becomes difficult.

Courage taps you on the shoulder, inviting you to embark on a journey to heal from trauma. In this moment, you face a choice: let the resistance from fear hold you back, or commit to rising above fear and resistance to heal. By choosing commitment, you choose to move forward from your past, rather than remain stagnant—procrastinating—in a quest for perfection.

Having the courage to commit means dedicating your energy and focus to healing from trauma despite feeling scared or unmotivated. It means sticking to a routine that includes good habits, like eating well to break the Trifecta Effect, staying positive with your purpose, and setting clear boundaries to protect your energy—and the more you stick to these commitments, the more you turn them into habits. The courage to commit to healing from trauma helps build your ability to stay dedicated and reduces your susceptibility to fear and procrastination.

The Courage to Persevere

Healing from trauma is not easy. The odds of facing challenges on your healing journey are high. But if you only proceeded when circumstances were favorable, you would never accomplish anything worthwhile. You have to have the courage to persevere.

Persevering doesn't mean you're immune to setbacks, that you don't get knocked down, or that you don't slip up when bad things happen to you. It means accepting that struggling is a part of existing. It's deciding to continue through setbacks, resistance, and fear. It's staying committed to healing even when it feels impossible.

Any progress, no matter how small, is valuable. Perseverance means that, instead of sitting back and waiting for a better time—procrastinating—you continue to move forward, one step at a time. You act even when it doesn't seem like the "perfect" time to do so.

Persevering through resistance is a powerful way to learn and grow from your experiences. Instead of remaining stagnant and accepting your current situation, you develop resilience and strength. You become better equipped to handle stress and adapt to new situations, which will serve you well in the future.

The courage to persevere through setbacks separates those who heal from trauma from those who remain stuck in their pain. It takes perseverance to overcome challenging times and declare, "I won't give up." To affirm, "I will overcome any challenge that comes my way. I will heal." The courage to persevere keeps you on track on your healing journey, no matter what challenges life throws your way.

The Courage to Stay Truthful

If fear is often described as "False Evidence Appearing Real," then we can define truth as "True Reality Understood Through Honesty." Having the courage to stay truthful means being honest and authentic in the face of fear and resistance. It involves upholding your values and beliefs even when it is difficult or risky to do so. Being honest with yourself on your healing journey about your progress and setbacks allows you to make realistic assessments and adjustments. By being honest about your progress and setbacks, you can stay focused on practical, incremental steps rather than getting stuck in the paralysis of perfectionism. This keeps you accountable for your actions and progress and builds your confidence that you can rely on yourself in challenging situations.

The courage to stay truthful helps us reduce the pressure from resistance that often leads to procrastination. When we are honest with ourselves, we clearly see the fear and resistance behind our delays. We shift from hiding behind seeking perfection to focusing on making steady progress.

Truth fundamentally strengthens our character. Each time we choose truth, we reinforce our integrity and build confidence in our ability to handle life's complexities. However, staying truthful is not without its challenges. Being honest sometimes means facing uncomfortable truths about ourselves or risking displeasure from others. These moments can feel daunting. Yet, it is through our courage to stay truthful despite our trials that we reinforce our commitment to living authentically and healing from trauma.

The Courage to Answer the Call

The hero's journey is a classic story pattern in which a main character embarks on an unexpected adventure, with courage as the central theme. Healing from trauma mirrors this journey. In this story, *you* are the hero. You are the main character who must answer "the call," the first stage of the hero's journey. This call manifests as a deep-seated feeling that something in your life needs to change.

Taking on the hero's journey requires facing your fears, stepping outside of your comfort zone, and embracing vulnerability and openness to change. Above all, it demands bravery.

Typically, the call to adventure is met with what is known as the *refusal of the call*. The resistance born from fear leads many to say no to the call, avoiding confrontation with their fears and the unknown. This refusal keeps them locked in "freeze" mode. It holds them back from healing.

How do you find the courage to answer the call? It begins by accepting a simple truth: no one is coming to save you. If no help is on the way, then who will step in? The answer is *you*. You are the one who must become brave. Because without the bravery to confront and overcome your own resistance, there's a risk that the old you might resurface, refusing the call and the opportunity to heal from trauma.

My client Andrew arrived in New Jersey for a retreat I hosted, ready for change and eager to heal and embrace a new version of himself. By the last day, he was motivated to apply the holistic health practices he had learned, and he prepared to return home as his new self. But as he was about to leave, I felt compelled to remind him, "Hey, remember, this is just the beginning. It's easy to feel inspired when you step out of your environment; the real journey of becoming the new you starts now."

While coaching him through the initial steps of healing—the same ones outlined in previous chapters—was straightforward, he still had to overcome his fear to answer the call. Despite dedicating ten years to his healing journey, Andrew had yet to fully embrace it.

Andrew knew what he needed to do. He knew eating healthy was not only good for his physical health but also for sustaining better energy. He also knew his purpose. But like most who face the unknown, he felt "stuck." He struggled with perfectionism and procrastination. And he was unaware of how his resistance stemmed from fear, which led him to believe he was irreparably broken.

The next step for Andrew after leaving my retreat was to trust himself and build the courage to answer the call. He realized that he had been subconsciously hoping someone else would come along and do the healing for him. He thought retreats, courses, and self-help books were the answer. Eventually, he came to understand that he had to save himself.

He realized that his past failures were not a reflection of his inadequacy. Instead, they stemmed from a lack of understanding about where his resistance came from. This left him vulnerable to procrastination whenever he hit an obstacle along his healing journey, and led him to see his failures as a lack of perfection. Today Andrew no longer views himself as broken. Instead, he sees obstacles as opportunities for learning and growth, approaching them with a positive mindset and determination. The courage Andrew developed gave him the confidence to do something he never thought he was able to do, which we will learn more about in Chapter 10.

Fear will always find a way to make itself known. Will we let it stop us from answering the call? Will we leave the phone ringing? Or, like Andrew, will we answer, finding the courage to heal?

REFUSING THE CALL

When we do not become courageous in the face of fear, perfection and procrastination prevent us from taking decisive action toward healing. We become afraid to move forward and let go of the past. We fear success because we understand that success means making changes in our lives, some of which require addressing parts of ourselves we've either avoided or are embarrassed by.

My friend, college roommate, and teammate, Aris Scott, was a star on the football field. He was gifted, determined, and hardworking. Though he was raised on the streets of Harrisburg, Pennsylvania, under circumstances much like my own, his future looked promising. After college, while I moved to New York to pursue my purpose, Aris remained at school and trained for the NFL. Yet, when draft night came, his name was not called.

His NFL dreams over, Aris didn't answer the call to move beyond his football career. He clung to the prospect of a professional sports career, unaware that his attachment to his old self was causing him deep pain, and he returned to the only life he knew—the streets.

As I moved on from my past, from football to coaching, my new career flourished, and Aris reached out and expressed pride in my accomplishments. It reminded me of our college dialogues about ambition and success, and the guilt of my success weighed on me, knowing Aris faced hardships. When I established my life in Los Angeles a few years later, Aris reached out in a call that I anticipated with warmth, ready for a conversation reminiscent of our college days. Instead, Aris confided, "I'm struggling, bro. For the first time, thoughts of ending it all have crossed my mind. I'm at rock bottom."

This shattered me. I assured him, "We'll get you the help you need." I flew him to LA.

Our days began with managing his sensitive nervous system, helping him find his purpose, and, most importantly, teaching him how to conquer fear and let go of his past self. Aris struggled to leave behind those who were not on his dream team, unaware that they were a negative influence on him. He was constantly being reminded of how he was supposed to be a professional football player, instead of being inspired to move forward.

Even when Aris found a new purpose, becoming a real estate agent, he procrastinated in taking action. He doubted his ability to leave his past dream behind and embrace this new direction. He kept waiting for the perfect moment to make the transition. I helped Aris craft a simple plan to secure his real estate license. And Aris committed to harnessing the courage for transformation.

Now, Aris is a leading real estate agent, on a trajectory to be one of the best in the nation. These days his social media reflects a different kind of victory than it did in his college days. He's suited up, not for game day, but for his clients, closing deals and creating new beginnings for himself and others.

Aris refused the call to embark on his healing journey because he wasn't honest with himself about the need to let go of his past self and those around him who didn't support his new purpose. Letting go of the old you isn't about forgetting. It's about having the courage to embrace the new and acknowledging that the change growth often requires might initially feel uncomfortable.

You may not succeed the first time you answer the call. Results are never guaranteed. Yet it's crucial to make the attempt, because the one thing you can be sure of is that inaction will inevitably lead to failure. By taking that first step on your hero's journey, you pave the way for success and personal growth. Embrace that journey, knowing that the effort brings you closer to healing from trauma, regardless of the immediate outcome.

FROM STAGNATION TO MOMENTUM

It's easier to yield to resistance than to muster the courage to overcome it. However, while avoiding resistance might seem easier in the moment, it creates more pain in the long run.

Let's say you come to me wanting to get stronger in the gym. I'll introduce resistance training to challenge your body, and then, as you master each workout, I'll add more reps, more sets, and heavier weights over time. Why? The body adapts to stress. Without increased resistance, your strength plateaus and progress halts. Perseverance through resistance is what leads to growth.

Maybe that sounds hard or painful. It can be. But avoiding the gym leads to a different pain altogether—the pain of weakened muscles, joint discomfort, poor posture, and a buildup of negative emotions. Avoiding the resistance of fear simply trades short-term comfort for long-term pain. We must decide which we'd rather face: the pain of perseverance or the pain of stagnation.

Courage generates momentum. The more we push through resistance, the stronger and more resilient we become. As we consistently use courage to confront these challenges, overcoming fear gradually becomes more familiar and less daunting. We rewire our sensations, feelings, thoughts, and perceptions as we journey into the unknown. Subconsciously, we become ready to face fear whenever it infiltrates our consciousness, armed with the knowledge that fear and resistance are not obstacles but opportunities for growth—chances to evolve into the best versions of ourselves.

9

HOLISTIC HEALING THROUGH STRENGTH TRAINING

For the first few years of my life, I was raised by my grand-mothers, going back and forth between their homes. My father's mother had an apartment, and my mother's mother lived in the Holland Gardens projects. During this period, my mother struggled with her own challenges. After her release from prison, she was on probation. She attended rehab and tried to get her life back on track so she could get custody of my siblings and me. After showing consistent improvement, the state of New Jersey granted my mother custody, a Section 8 housing voucher, and welfare. When I was eight years old, we moved with her to a town called Bayonne. Unfortunately, things quickly declined for us.

137

My mother began seeing a man named Krime, a tall, muscular African-American man with cornrows and a domineering presence. Soon after entering our lives, he moved in and immediately imposed his rules on our household. Among those rules was the demand that we call him dad. Angry and uncomfortable with that, I confronted him, telling him, "I have a father, and you're not him. I won't call you dad."

In response, he violently lifted me against the wall and landed a sucker punch to my stomach, forcing the air out of me. "If you ever talk back to me," he said in a low, dangerous tone, "I'll beat yo ass, boy."

My older brother, then ten years old, rushed over to protect me, but Krime just let go of me and turned his anger onto my brother. I turned to my mother, my eyes pleading for her to intervene, but she just stood there, offering no help or comfort.

I tried to help my brother, but Krime's strength was too much. He pushed me aside and kept on hitting us. When he was done, he made us sit on the couch and went over his rules again. There we were, bleeding, bruised, our shirts torn, trying to catch our breath. But I wasn't going to let him have the last word.

"I'm going to tell my father about this," I warned. "You're going to regret this."

In Jersey City, my father's street reputation was legendary. No one in their right mind would dare lay a hand on me, knowing the kind of men my father and uncles were. But Krime just strolled to the kitchen and seized the largest knife we owned. He returned, sat down, and, pointing the blade at my older brother and me, said, "If you ever tell your father, or anyone for that matter, about what happens in this house, I'll kill your mother first. Then, I'll come for all of you."

Given Krime's past and the way he said it, I had no doubt he meant every word. After all, the nickname "Krime" wasn't given lightly.

The beatings from Krime lasted months, and his rules were cemented in our household. While the boys got beaten by Krime, my older sister got hers from my mother. None of the rules Krime imposed were familiar to me. Neither my father nor any other man in my family had ever subjected me to such treatment, especially when it came to beatings. My father and uncles were wise men. They allowed me to make mistakes, trusting that, when I needed to, I would turn to them for advice and life lessons. Krime's abusive behavior ensured I'd never rely on him for anything.

Krime had this rule that we hold his hand in public. It felt demeaning and uncomfortable. Once, after school, he reached out to take my hand in front of my teacher and classmates. I immediately pulled away. He locked eyes with me, a cold, unblinking stare that lasted what felt like an eternity.

Without breaking his gaze, he grabbed my arm and said, "Let's go." I knew immediately what awaited me. When we reached the apartment, Krime unleashed on me the most severe beating I had ever endured.

Afterward, Krime decided that I was no longer allowed to stay at the apartment. He demanded I leave, and because my younger brother Brandon and I shared the same father, Krime made him leave, too. My older brother's and sister's biological father wasn't present in their lives, so they had no choice but to stay behind. He yanked Brandon and me out of the apartment. Once again, my mother remained silent.

At my father's door in Jersey City, where he shared an apartment with a roommate, Krime crouched down to our eye level. "Remember what I told you two," he hissed. "If you spill a word to your dad about what happens in my house, first your mother will die. Then, I'll get your brother and sister. And after that, you two are next." Rising to his full height, he straightened his shirt and knocked sharply.

My father opened the door, taken aback to find us there. He looked at me, noticing my body language and ripped-up shirt, Brandon's fearful eyes, and my own visible distress. "Nate," he began, his voice thick with concern, "what the hell happened?" But before I could muster an answer, Krime jumped in, "They got into a fight. Your boys have been acting out, picking fights at school almost daily. They've turned into little thugs in Bayonne. They need to be with you right now." With that, he turned on his heel and walked away.

My father took Brandon and me by the hand, gently closing the door behind us. He guided us to sit down, his eyes searching ours. "Tell me what happened," he urged. He was confident in the values he had instilled in us, and the story about us being thugs didn't match that.

I met my father's gaze, trying to muster the strength to recount the events at my mother's house, but the words wouldn't come out. It was as though I had floated out of my body. The ability to articulate my pain escaped me. My breathing grew rapid, my body trembled, and, even as I tried to keep a straight face, tears welled up and streamed down. More than anything, I wanted to tell my father everything, but the weight of fear and the possibility of endangering my mother with the truth made me hold my tongue.

STUCK ON PAUSE

The trauma Krime had inflicted had replaced my fight-or-flight response with something more paralyzing: *freeze* mode. Before, I would confront challenges head-on. Now, when I was presented with stress or threats, I simply couldn't move, communicate, or defend myself. Sometimes, this can feel similar to the resistance that arises from fear, which we discussed in the previous chapter. But this state of paralysis is different. It's a subconscious response that stems from trauma—what psychologists call immobilization.

Immobilization is a frequent response when facing overwhelming stress or danger, especially in situations where you can't fight back or escape, such as childhood trauma involving parents or caregivers. It can also happen when experiencing abusive relationships or bullying, or when witnessing violence. Instead of fighting or fleeing, you become paralyzed—you freeze. It's an involuntary reaction the body instinctively uses to protect itself when it feels there is no other hope for survival. It's similar to a small bird playing dead in the face of a predator, conserving energy and hoping to go unnoticed.

In the aftermath of trauma, immobilization can become a subconscious, automatic reaction whenever our sensitive nervous system experiences stress levels so high that it feels helpless. Instead of our nervous system increasing our heart rate and breathing, with immobilization, our heart rate slows down, and our breathing can become very shallow or even stop briefly. We are filled with stress hormones and instinctively want to move in some way—fighting or fleeing—but instead become stuck on pause.

Immobilization plays a significant role in one of the biggest issues mentioned by new clients: knowing what to do but not doing it. Even though we understand the importance of eating better, getting more rest, exercising, and setting boundaries with our purpose, we can feel so overloaded with stress that we subconsciously respond by *freezing*.

When we are unable to take action despite knowing what needs to be done, it can lead to feelings of helplessness and frustration. Repeatedly failing to meet our own expectations or the expectations of others in our relationships and work can erode our self-esteem. We start to doubt our abilities and question our self-worth. The sense of paralysis and inability to control our responses to stress can make us feel *weak* and inadequate. Over time, this can significantly diminish our confidence and self-worth.

This diminished confidence can manifest in various ways. It can cause us to withdraw from social interactions, isolating ourselves from friends, family, and colleagues. This isolation reinforces feelings of loneliness and inadequacy, further diminishing our confidence. It also fosters negative self-talk. Unaware of the way we are subconsciously wired to freeze in response to stress, we engage in self-criticism, believing we are not taking action toward our goals, social interactions, and work responsibilities because we are unmotivated, incompetent, or lazy. This habit of doubting our abilities and worth convinces us that we are incapable of overcoming challenges or achieving our goals.

Immobilization has an impact on us physically as well. The lack of confidence that immobilization creates may cause us to walk with a slouched posture, avoid eye contact, and display nervous behaviors, signaling our lack of confidence in ourselves to others. This body language can perpetuate a cycle of low self-esteem, as our physical state reflects and reinforces our mental state.

Hobbies, passions, and even basic self-care begin to feel like insurmountable tasks. This loss of interest not only deprives us of pleasure but also robs us of opportunities to build competence and confidence through engagement and achievement. When we stop engaging in activities that once brought us joy, we miss out on the positive reinforcement and sense of accomplishment that come from pursuing our interests.

As you can see, freeze mode can make us feel trapped and powerless—and the positive self-talk and courage used to transform our self-perspective and overcome fear, which we discussed in previous chapters, may not be enough to break free. We cannot talk or convince our way out of this frozen, "paused" state.

So, how can we overcome "freeze mode" and move beyond this paralysis to make true progress? The answer lies in full-body *mobilization*. This involves moving the body, reactivating the muscles for strength, reconnecting with our surroundings, and getting the mind-body connection back online. Physical movement helps unlock us from paralysis, allowing us to fully engage with the world around us and regain control over our actions.

It's helped many of my clients break through their paused state, and it's what helped me break through my immobilization, too.

FROM STUCK TO STRONG

After two years, my mother and Krime parted ways, and when my mother's lease in Bayonne ended, she relocated to Jersey City Heights. My brother Brandon and I moved back in with her. Unfortunately, my mother started using again. I hadn't realized my mother was an addict until then. I was ten years old.

During this time, my mother started dating a man named Joe, a Puerto Rican who had just gotten out of prison. With his massive build, he resembled the Hulk, and I braced myself for a repeat of the challenges I faced with Krime. But to my surprise, Joe was different. He turned out to be the best stepfather I could have asked for. Apart from my father, he was the first man who genuinely loved and cared for my mother and her kids.

Joe was all about discipline. Every morning, while my mother still slept, he would make his side of the bed, slip into his tank top and long johns, and head straight to the park for his workout. I was definitely impressed by his discipline, but it was his physique that truly captivated me. He had the build of a superhero and carried himself with undeniable confidence. I wanted to emulate that.

"Yo, Joe," I started.

He looked over. "What's up, Papi?"

"How'd you get so strong? How'd you build all those muscles?" I asked.

"Calisthenics," he answered with a grin.

I wrinkled my brow. "What's calisthenics?"

"It's training by using your own body weight, Papi," he explained.

"So, you never used weights or anything?" I asked.

He shook his head. "No, Papi. In prison, we didn't have weights. But we did have pull-up and dip bars. We used those and our body weight to build strength and muscle."

I felt inspired and eager to learn more. I decided to get up early the next day to join Joe at the park. As we arrived, I noticed that a few of his friends, who had also recently been released from prison, were already there. Each one held a blue coffee cup from the local bodega. As we entered the playground, they put down their cups, put on construction gloves, and started to work out. They used the monkey bars for pull-ups, and the playground climbers for dips. I saw how easy it was for them to lift their own bodyweight and perform these exercises. I knew I couldn't do it, and I became discouraged.

When it was my turn to go, I hesitated, but one of Joe's friends said, "Come on, little man, you got this. We're here to assist you." They refused to let me see myself as the chubby kid who could barely manage to jump. They supported me through my pull-ups, literally holding my feet, and shouted encouragement as I struggled with my push-ups. Through their unwavering belief in me, they painted a picture of a future where I was strong and courageous.

After about fifteen minutes into our session, the raw emotions of the older men began to emerge. They shouted affirmations as they pushed through their workout: "I won't back down here, and I won't back down in life!" Their conversations shifted to the scars left by trauma, and they discussed the importance of breathing during your workout to release pent-up pain and trauma.

I began to realize that these workouts were not solely about physical strength. They represented therapy, peer support, and motivation, all rolled into one. These men faced tremendous barriers due to their criminal records. They were unable to travel freely or pursue certain jobs, and this was their way of coping. They had found a way to confront trauma, loneliness, and heartache. This was their unique route to healing and transformation, a path carved from the very heart of the ghetto.

I left that workout with an unfamiliar confidence surging through me. More than that, I felt in control—of my thoughts, my body, and my emotions. For the first time in two years, I was free of the paralyzing freeze mode I'd been stuck in since Krime. I had stumbled onto a way out—full-body mobilization.

Joe and his friends taught me how to transform the trauma I carried by taking ownership of my body through strength training. This process empowered me, allowing me to gain strength, confidence, and the ability to take initiative in shaping and recreating my life.

As I engaged more deeply in regular workouts, I discovered that physical movement was more than just exercise—it was a way to reconnect with my mind and body and, in turn, my sense of self. The physical strength I gained mirrored the mental resilience I was building. I started to stand taller, both literally and metaphorically. The confidence I developed through strength training spilled over into my daily interactions. I no longer froze in the face of stress or pressure. Instead, I again confronted challenges head-on, knowing I had the strength to overcome them.

Joe and his friends, who had faced significant challenges themselves, taught me that physical training could serve as a catalyst for reclaiming control. Their experiences showed that, despite their pasts, they could still take charge of their bodies and lives—and they inspired me to do the same.

HEALING IMMOBILIZATION WITH THE THIRD LAYER OF ENERGY

As you may remember, the five layers of energy begin with the nervous system and move to the organs and glands, especially the hypothalamus, pituitary, and adrenal glands. When we experience stress or trauma, these glands prepare our muscles—the third layer—for fight or flight. Our stress hormones and physical responses reinforce emotional reactions, making us feel anxious or upset—the fourth layer of energy. Over time, these repeated reactions impact the fifth layer of energy, our subconscious, which can keep us in survival mode.

In the plan laid out by this book, we begin with healing the first layer of energy—our sensitive nervous system—by breaking the Trifecta Effect, and then taking steps to heal the rest of the layers of energy. This approach is very effective for healing our sensitive nervous system that is primed for fighting or fleeing, helping our autonomic nervous system response. But when it comes to overcoming immobilization, being stuck in "freeze mode," starting with the third layer of energy—the muscular system—may be the best approach.

Addressing immobilization with strength training isn't just about addressing physical stagnation. It's about improving our psychological state, too. Strength training allows us to use the power of our body to positively affect our minds by releasing *endorphins*, which improve mood and mental clarity.

When we are stuck on pause, with decreased heart rate and shallow breathing, strength training speeds them up, helping us reconnect to our psychological stress response. In other words, we regain the ability of fight or flight.

If we fail to overcome immobilization, the flood of stress hormones with no release through fight or flight leaves us with a muscular system that is tight and tense. With elevated stress hormones and a muscular system stuck on pause, we risk a buildup of emotions. When we address the physical immobility created by freeze mode through strength training, tight muscles are released and physical tension is alleviated.

Think of your body like a sponge soaked with water. The water inside represents your emotions. Just like squeezing the sponge releases water, strengthening and moving tight muscles helps release emotions. Think of how Joe and his friends began to express their emotions during our training sessions, or how, after you get a massage or do yoga, you often feel lighter and more at ease.

Strength training also improves your posture by turning once tense and rigid muscles strong and flexible, which improves physical stability. This also impacts your emotional state. Despite your efforts to hide or move beyond a traumatic past or chronic stress, your body language often reveals the struggles you carry within. Research shows that individuals with poor posture not only experience more negative emotions but also increased signs of low confidence, sadness, and fear in response to stress.[18]

Good posture—standing upright, with chest tall and shoulders back—is beneficial for your emotional state and helps build resilience to stress. It also affects how others see you. Standing with your chest forward instead of slouching projects self-assurance, self-esteem, and a positive attitude.

In short, using strength training to overcome immobilization will reengage the body's natural stress responses. As the body becomes more capable and resilient, the mind follows suit, breaking free from the patterns of paralysis and promoting a sense of control and confidence.

KEEPING EXERCISE SIMPLE WITH COMPOUND EXERCISES

When you start incorporating strength training, you can begin the same way I did with Joe and his friends: keeping exercise simple by focusing on compound exercises.

Compound exercises are movements that engage multiple muscle groups simultaneously. For example, a squat activates your core, quads, hamstrings, glutes, calf muscles, *and* hip flexors, and it also promotes overall body coordination and balance. In contrast, isolation exercises like a bicep curl specifically target one muscle group. Compound exercises are superior for improving and maintaining good posture because they mimic natural movements and distribute the workload across various muscles. This ensures more balanced and functional strength that supports proper body alignment.

Compound exercises are particularly beneficial for beginners because they provide a comprehensive workout with fewer movements, making building a balanced and strong body less complicated. By focusing on compound exercises, you can achieve more significant results in less time compared to isolation exercises.

I've separated the exercises that follow into two levels to provide a clear path as you progress. Level One is calisthenics, what I used to do with Joe. Calisthenics, which use a person's body weight to perform exercises, engages multiple muscle groups simultaneously and requires little to no equipment. This allows you to do these exercises at home if you are hesitant about going to the gym.

Level Two is weight training, which involves using external resistance, such as free weights, resistance bands, or machines, to build muscle mass and strength. Like calisthenics, strength training also engages multiple muscle groups, but with added resistance you can target and overload specific muscles more effectively.

Once you've improved strength and stability using your own body weight through calisthenics in Level One, you are ready to add external resistance for weight training in Level Two. This step-by-step approach ensures that you build a solid foundation before moving on to more challenging exercises, reducing the risk of injury and promoting long-term success.

In both Level One and Level Two, the objective is to aim for progressive overload—gradually increasing the level of difficulty over time. The goal is to avoid hitting plateaus, where your body becomes accustomed to the exercises and no longer makes progress, so you continue to build muscle and strength effectively.

Level One: Calisthenics

Perform the following exercises in a circuit, rotating through each exercise from number 1 to number 6, then starting back at number 1. Once you have finished all six exercises in a row, you have completed one set of the circuit. Allow a minimum of 60 seconds of rest between each exercise. If you can't perform an exercise due to difficulty or physical limitations, you can modify it as suggested or skip it, removing it from your circuit.

1. **Push-Ups:** Start in a plank position with your hands shoulder-width apart. Lower your body until your chest nearly touches the floor, then push back up to the starting position. For modifications, try knee push-ups or wall push-ups.

2. **Lunges:** Stand with your feet hip-width apart. Step forward with one leg and lower your hips to drop your back knee toward the ground, keeping your front knee behind your toes. Push back to the starting position and repeat with the other leg. For a less intense version, reduce the depth of the lunge.

3. **Pull-Ups:** Grip a pull-up bar with your hands shoulder-width apart and palms facing away from you. Pull your body up until your chin is above the bar, then lower yourself back down. If pull-ups are too challenging, loop a resistance band around the bar and place one foot or knee into the band for assistance, or perform negative pull-ups by starting with your chin above the bar and slowly lowering down.

4. **Squats:** Stand with your feet shoulder-width apart, toes pointing slightly outward. Bend your knees and lower your hips as if sitting back into a chair, keeping your chest up and back straight. Return to standing. To modify, perform the squat with a bench or chair to control the depth.

5. **Side Lunges:** Start with your feet together, holding your hands in front of your chest for balance. Step out to the side with one leg, bending the knee of the leg you stepped out with while keeping the other leg straight. Push back to

the starting position, and repeat on the other side. For an easier version, reduce the step width.

6. Sit-Ups: Lie on your back with your knees bent and feet flat on the floor. Cross your arms over your chest or place your fingertips behind your ears. Lift your upper body all the way up toward your knees, keeping your back straight, then slowly lower it back down. For a modification, try crunches or half sit-ups.

For optimal results, complete three sets of this circuit, starting with five reps per exercise. When you can successfully complete each step with five reps, progress to eight, then ten, then twelve, then fifteen, and finally twenty. Once you're able to perform three sets of twenty reps for this circuit, you have two options: increase the circuit sets from three to four, or add a weight vest. If you choose the latter, reset to the beginning with three sets of five reps and work your way back up to three sets of twenty reps. After achieving three sets of twenty reps with the vest, you can add more weight to the vest or increase the sets to four.

Once you're able to complete at least three circuit sets of ten reps of each exercise, you can, if you feel ready for more challenge, move on to Level Two—weight training.

Level Two: Weight Training

The following exercises emphasize the use of dumbbells, small bars with equal weights on each side. For each exercise, you'll use a dumbbell in each hand (two dumbbells per exercise). As a beginner transitioning from calisthenics, start with a light weight that allows you to perform each exercise with proper form. A good starting point is typically 5 pounds. The most important factor in choosing a starting weight, or moving up in weight, is your ability to maintain good form throughout the set.

Begin with three sets of eight reps per exercise, then progress to three sets of ten reps, to three sets of twelve reps, and finally to three sets of fifteen reps. Upon achieving three sets of fifteen reps, increase the weight of each dumbbell by 5 pounds, starting again at three sets of eight reps. Once you can complete three sets of fifteen reps with the increased weight, you can either add another set to your routine, making it four sets, or increase the weight again by 5 pounds and reset to three sets of eight reps.

In this level, exercises are paired into groups. Start with Group One, and after completing all sets for each exercise, proceed to the next group until all are completed. Focus on completing all sets and reps for one group before moving on to the next. Allow a minimum of 90 seconds of rest between exercises within a group and 2 to 3 minutes of rest between groups. If you are unable to perform a specific exercise, skip it and continue with the remaining exercises in the group.

Group One

Dumbbell Overhead Press: Stand with feet shoulder-width apart, holding a dumbbell in each hand at shoulder level with your palms facing in. Press the dumbbells upward until your arms are fully extended overhead. Lower them back to shoulder level.

Dumbbell Back Row: Holding a dumbbell in each hand with palms facing each other, bend forward at the waist, keeping your back straight. With your arms extended down from your shoulders, pull the dumbbells toward your hips, squeezing your shoulder blades together. Lower the dumbbells back down.

Group Two

Dumbbell Lunges: Stand upright holding a dumbbell in each hand. Step forward with one leg and lower your hips to drop your back knee toward the ground, keeping your front knee behind your toes. Push back to the starting position and repeat with the other leg.

Dumbbell Side Lunges: Stand with feet together, holding a dumbbell in each hand. Step out to the side with one leg, bending the knee of the leg you stepped out with while keeping the other leg straight. Push back to the starting position and repeat on the other side.

Group Three

Dumbbell Bench Press: Lie on your back on a bench with a dumbbell in each hand, arms extended above your chest. With your palms facing each other, lower the dumbbells to chest level, keeping your elbows at a 45-degree angle to your body. Then press the dumbbells back up to the starting position.

Dumbbell Sit-Ups: Lie on your back with knees bent and feet flat on the ground. Hold a single dumbbell at your chest with a hand on each end, keeping your elbows close to your sides. Perform a sit-up by lifting your upper body toward your knees, keeping the dumbbell close to your chest. Lower back down and repeat.

Dumbbell Squats: Stand with feet shoulder-width apart, holding a dumbbell in each hand at your sides with your palms facing in. Bend your knees and lower your hips as if sitting back into a chair, keeping your chest up and back straight. Return to standing.

Once you can complete at least three sets of ten reps with 20 pounds for each exercise, you can add reps, sets, and weight, or you can blend Level One and Level Two training, focusing on progressive overload for both. Alternatively, you can move on to performing these exercises with a barbell for an added challenge.

*

HOLISTIC HEALING THROUGH STRENGTH TRAINING

Incorporating strength training into your routine is a tremendous return on investment, providing both physical and mental benefits that transform your life. It helps unlock paralysis, allowing you to fully engage with the world and regain control over your actions, while providing a channel for expressing built-up and stagnant emotions. It rewires three key layers of energy: the muscular system, the nervous system, and emotions. Embracing this powerful tool transforms both your body and mind, leading to a more confident, empowered self. This mental clarity then spills over into other areas of life, making it easier to make purposeful decisions and set healthy boundaries.

As usual, consistency is key. The greater our consistency, the more effectively we can integrate these practices into the fifth layer of energy—the subconscious.

Remember, each of the five layers of energy influences the next, either positively or negatively. Addressing trauma and chronic stress by isolating a single energy layer may offer temporary relief for specific situations, but it does not ensure long-lasting results. Adopting a holistic approach that includes strength training promotes overall well-being and empowers you to pursue opportunities as your authentic self.

10

THE ONE PERCENTER

I want to take a moment to talk particularly to readers who are overcoming generational trauma and poverty. Maybe you're the first in your family to achieve things nobody else has, or maybe you're inspired to be that pioneer. Pause to reflect on how far you've come. Consider everything you've accomplished, despite the odds being stacked against you. Think about how few people have accomplished what you already have. I call people like us One Percenters—people who defeated the odds that kept 99 percent of our peers from breaking out of their generational cycles. But not you. You've shattered those limits and risen above the challenges. You are a One Percenter, someone on a mission to overcome generational trauma and poverty.

Take my upbringing as an example: both of my parents grew up in poverty, struggled with addiction, never graduated from high school, and have health issues. My older siblings face similar challenges. Yet, here I stand, distinct and apart.

The likelihood of me avoiding welfare, graduating from high school and college, steering clear of gangs, not having a child at a young age, and remaining free from substance addiction was incredibly slim. In fact, if you combine all the statistics, my chances were close to, if not less than, 1 percent. Additionally, I became the first Division I football player in my school's history. With only about 130 Division I programs, each offering eighty-five scholarships, there are roughly 11,000 scholarship Division I football players out there. Considering there are approximately 1.1 million high school football players, my odds of achieving this were exactly 1 percent.

Maybe we could attribute our success to luck, except our beating the odds doesn't just happen once; it's a trend that often continues without us recognizing it. We are so focused on moving on to the next goal, stuck in survival mode long after we made it through, that we don't take the time to reflect on how far we've come. Because we fear failing, we spend most of our time focusing on what we have done wrong, rather than seeing our achievements. We struggle with seeing them because no one has recognized and complimented us for what we've achieved. But, if you take the time to research the odds of your successes, I bet you'll find the same thing that I did: you are far more resilient and capable than you give yourself credit for.

However, for most One Percenters, progress often slows down as we get older—usually by our late twenties to early thirties. That's when we start to notice our health issues worsening. So, why do some of us stop moving forward and overcoming the odds?

Maybe fatigue and brain fog prevent us from staying consistent with our purpose. Or maybe digestive issues and the discomfort of bloating and muscular pain make it difficult to pursue our dreams. These symptoms can feel surprising to One Percenters because, prior to experiencing these health issues, our stress hormones kept us hyperfocused on survival, which numbed us to the negative impacts our sensitive nervous systems were having on our body.

At first, we perceived ourselves as having a strong mindset and body that never got tired. We thought we could push through any challenge. This confidence is the reason some One Percenters never ask for help; we're used to doing it all. But as One Percenters age, our stress levels increase. The Trifecta Effect is triggered more frequently by new responsibilities, including bills, work, and the absence of personal time to reflect and react to adversity. We feel guilty about protecting our energy, fearing that saying no might cause us to lose our loved ones. This makes us feel even more isolated, and sacrificing our energy leaves us feeling drained.

This level of stress creates an overwhelming cycle of unhappiness and poor health. It starts to extinguish the fire we once had for our goals in life. It pushes us further away from our purpose and from beating the odds that are stacked against us.

The One Percenter—you—needs to be understood, seen, and reminded that your healing is vitally important. Whether you realize it or not, you are here to change the trajectory of your family's paradigm. The same generational traumas and curses have been passed through your grandparents to your parents, and from your parents to you and your siblings. If this cycle is not broken, your family will continue to struggle. When you heal, you can forgive and help heal the generation before you, but more importantly, you can be an example for the next generation.

EMBRACING *YOUR* AUTHENTIC SELF

Authenticity is about embracing your unique qualities, owning your vulnerabilities, and stepping into the light as the incredible person you are. It's a journey—one that requires self-reflection, self-love, and a willingness to let go of masks that no longer serve you. When you embrace authenticity, you unlock the power to form deeper, more meaningful connections. You invite genuine relationships into your life, where you are loved and appreciated for your true self. This opens the door to a life filled with purpose and fulfillment, where every step you take resonates with your core values and purpose. Embracing your authentic self allows you to live boldly and unapologetically, as the extraordinary individual you were always meant to be.

Most of my clients hesitate at first to follow their deepest desires because these desires differ from what their peers, families, or society at large believe they should want. This hesitation is understandable; stepping outside the norm can feel risky and uncomfortable. We worry about judgment, rejection, or the loss of security that comes from fitting in. However, embracing your authentic self means recognizing that these desires are a true reflection of who you are and what you are capable of achieving.

Take, for example, Andrew, whom you met in Chapter 8. Andrew grew up in a cult in Florida, where every day was consumed by religious study. He was never permitted to leave the confines of the community he was brought up in. Nonetheless, he harbored a strong conviction that he could find success in the business realm. But whenever he dared to share his dreams with members of his community, he was immediately dismissed. The thought of leaving the cult presented itself as an insurmountable challenge; doing so meant jeopardizing his safety and security.

Andrew battled insecurities and struggled with his weight from a young age. Despite his diet and exercise efforts, the results he longed for eluded him. What Andrew didn't realize was that his sensitive nervous system, shaped by the abuse he endured, played a significant role in his weight issues. Yet his weight was not his primary concern; his sexuality was. Andrew was afraid to reveal to his family that he was gay, aware that coming out could expose him to further abuse and rejection from his family and community. In their eyes, his sexuality was a sin.

So, Andrew wore a mask. He acted in ways that made others happy and allowed him to be accepted. He married a woman, and they had three children. Andrew appeared to have the American dream: a house, a spouse, children, and financial security. However, deep down, he harbored a desire to live his purpose and be his authentic self. In his mid-twenties, the mask Andrew had been wearing began to crack. He was unhappy and continued to struggle with his health. Finally, gathering his courage, Andrew revealed his truth: he told his family and community about his sexuality. He divorced his wife and left the confines he had known his entire life. He stepped into the unknown and faced the outside world without any guarantees of safety, security, or support.

Andrew made his way into the business world with no formal education. He climbed to the top of his company and became one of the top 1 percent of salesmen in the country. He was extremely proud of his accomplishments, but as the years went by, his sensitive nervous system began to adversely affect him. As his stress levels rose, so did his fears. In the business world, Andrew hesitated to be himself. He was afraid of judgment and that he wouldn't be accepted. These familiar fears were triggering the Trifecta Effect.

After years of trial and error in his attempts to reduce his stress and heal his health issues, Andrew began to lose hope. Then, by chance, while scrolling through social media, Andrew saw one of my videos, and he reached out to connect with me. I had a workshop in Texas that month, several states away, and—driven to learn more about his sensitive nervous system—he flew in to attend.

As Andrew entered the workshop, I welcomed him with a hug and called him brother. I shared my gratitude for his effort to fly to Texas just to attend my one-day workshop. Andrew was deeply moved by the experience. He found himself surrounded by individuals like himself, all grappling with the aftermath of trauma. Andrew had moved from a strict community right into the fast-paced lifestyle of the business world. Both environments made Andrew feel like an outsider.

After the one-day workshop, Andrew applied to become a personal client. Whenever I take on a new client, I begin with what I call a three-day subconscious retreat. I spend eight hours a day with the client, teaching them in person everything I've discussed in this book. I decided to start this weekend differently with Andrew. I took him to meet my father.

Andrew had confided in me that he felt as though he never really had a family, and he never felt supported for who he truly is. He thought this feeling was normal. Initially, this confused me, but I had to remind myself of his limited experience with the outside world. Andrew admired me for being my authentic self. He often asked how I found the courage to be true to myself without fear of judgment. What Andrew didn't know was that I, too, struggled with being my real self. It was my father who taught and showed me the importance of authenticity.

Whenever my father and I entered a store when I was a child, the store owners would follow us, believing my father would rob them. There were times we waited for hours at the bus stop to visit my grandmother, as bus drivers passed by without stopping for us. When I spent time with my mother's side of the family, and my father would visit, he was never allowed inside. I had to speak to him through the window. I always wondered why people were so cruel to my father. Then, as a teenager, I realized that my father never compromised who he truly was. Yes, he was a Black man, but more than that, he was a proud Black man who never wore a mask to hide. He didn't allow anyone to make him feel ashamed of who he was. Instead, he showed his pride every day by keeping his Black power fist pick in his Afro. He never was bothered by the judgment or rejection of others.

After Andrew's flight from Florida to New Jersey, I took him to my father's house where we all sat down to chat. I regarded Andrew as my brother, and I wanted to share my father with him—a parent who never judges but instead encourages you to be your true self. To clarify, I hadn't informed my father about Andrew's specific circumstances. I simply expressed my desire for one of my clients to meet him, and he was very welcoming.

Within the first few minutes of meeting him, my father gave Andrew the same advice he gave me anytime he sensed hesitation in being my authentic self: "There's only one of you. The creator made you like this. All your flaws are your true gifts; it's only when you embrace them that you can truly shine."

As Andrew and I returned to the car after our visit, he told me, tears in his eyes, "I never thought it was possible for someone who didn't know me to accept and understand me. Your father made me feel seen."

That weekend, Andrew not only learned how to rewire his mind, body, and emotions but also recognized it was time for a new purpose. He was inspired by the idea of producing online content to share his story with the world and establish a supportive community—a void he had felt deeply. Yet, his old self began to question this new direction, causing a wave of doubt that threatened to derail his Pursuit of Purpose.

I encouraged Andrew to take out his journal and list all his accomplishments. We then researched the statistics on the likelihood of overcoming the challenges he had faced; unsurprisingly, it turned out to be around 1 percent. At that moment, I seized the opportunity to remind Andrew that he is a One Percenter. He is someone who turns the seemingly impossible into the possible, but with one important caveat: *as long as he takes care of his sensitive nervous system.*

Today, Andrew is actively creating content, sharing his story, cultivating his community, and enjoying both happiness and health. His journey to happiness wasn't paved with financial gain, material possessions, or fame; rather, he found true happiness by healing his nervous system and embracing his authentic self.

THE ROLE OF FORGIVENESS IN HEALING

Part of becoming your authentic self is learning how to forgive yourself. Embracing who you truly are involves letting go of past mistakes and the guilt associated with them. Forgiveness is a crucial step in the healing process and allows you to move forward with confidence and self-acceptance. As a One Percenter, you are on a profound journey of healing and growth. As you rewire your sensations, feelings, thoughts, and perspectives, it fundamentally shifts the way you perceive the world around you—including your past. It opens a gateway to view trauma through a different lens and fosters a sense of understanding and acceptance toward people, events, and things that once caused you pain. By reevaluating past experiences from this new vantage point, you pave the way for forgiveness.

Forgiveness is a conscious, deliberate decision to release feelings of resentment or vengeance toward a person or event that has harmed you. It does not mean forgetting, condoning, or excusing the offense. Instead, it changes your relationship with past events and empowers you to embrace a future unburdened by them. It allows you to release past grievances and frees you from carrying the weight of anger and resentment. Forgiveness opens the path for new, healthier relationships—with yourself and others.

Forgiving Yourself

I have my own regrets. There were times when I didn't know how to control my mind, body, and emotions. After years of abuse and getting into fights, I became very reactive. I would attack others before they could attack me. I could have used other ways to deal with the situation, but I responded based on what I knew.

In my early years, I gave many of my teachers and some students problems. I responded to the laughter that was directed at me because of my learning disabilities by turning into the class clown. I wasn't looking for attention, exactly. The jokes I made were rooted in the fear of being exposed. Everyone became scared to make a joke about me because they knew I would clown them for the rest of the school year. I was reacting to the embarrassment I felt by embarrassing other students, disrupting class, and making things challenging for my teachers. I probably made jokes that hurt other students, something I deeply regret. Back then, I was blind to the deeper insecurities that drove my actions.

Think about things you have done to yourself or others that caused pain. Have you forgiven yourself? Are you still dealing with guilt and regret for mistakes you've made? Offer compassion to your past self. You were just responding based on what you knew at the time. Every experience is a learning opportunity, and hindsight offers us the clarity we didn't have before. We all need forgiveness, a second chance, because we are all human, trying our best to figure out this journey of life.

Forgiving Those Who Caused You Trauma

As we heal, our perspective shifts, not just on our own past behavior, but on that of others. This is why I forgave my mother.

People are usually taken aback when I tell them this. They wonder, "How could you forgive your mother after everything she did to you?" But as a child, curiosity about my mother's actions consumed me. I was intent on unraveling an explanation behind her actions, abuse, addiction, and abandonment. While others judged her behaviors, I saw through them to a more profound narrative. Gazing into her eyes, I recognized a soul that was both young and lost, misplaced and misunderstood. Spiritually, it often felt like our roles were reversed—that she was the child, and I was the adult.

My mother's story began in the Holland Gardens projects of Jersey City, New Jersey. She was a child without a father, raised by an abusive mother who struggled with alcoholism. My mother's childhood was deeply troubled, and the stories I was told about her upbringing, filled with severe trauma and battles with mental health disorders, including schizophrenia and bipolar disorder, have left me with an immense sense of gratitude for my own upbringing. In the 1970s, when she was growing up, mental health was largely misunderstood and neglected. She was "the crazy girl from the projects." Her mental health disorders were unseen and untreated, so she turned to recreational drugs for relief.

My mother didn't find mentorship that could lead her out of the ghetto, like I did. She kept her story to herself because, in her days, what happened at home was supposed to stay at home. Speaking up about her struggles would just get her into more trouble at home. And even if she had been brave enough to share, back then empathy was scarce; judgment was not. Help was not a button away—there were no cell phones, no internet to provide escape or comfort or understanding. She couldn't dive into the digital world for advice, couldn't find momentary peace in a song streaming from a phone, nor discover guidance through online videos. She had no Paul Chek to look up to, no virtual mentor to light her path, as I had.

My mother was forced to grow up fast. She began missing school due to the trauma she suffered at home, eventually dropping out before finishing middle school. During this difficult time, she trusted a teenage boy (my older siblings' father) who provided her with a sense of safety. A few years later, she became a mother at sixteen years old, which postponed her own healing process. With her mental health needs unaddressed, she did what she could to cope with life's challenges. Her reactions—abusive behavior, reaching for drugs—mirrored the only options she had ever learned. She was caught in a chaotic cycle, with a sensitive nervous system that disconnected her mind from her emotions. Her life was just too difficult for her to navigate successfully.

As a child, I never understood why my mother couldn't quit her drug addiction. If she just got clean, I thought, she would stop being abusive toward my siblings and me, and we could finally have a normal household. As I grew and healed, my perspective on my mother shifted. I learned how challenging life can be when you lack resources and are dealing with a traumatic past and a sensitive nervous system. Instead of judging her for her abuse and abandonment, I came to understand why she is the way she is. This understanding has led me to forgiveness.

Have your parents or guardians caused you pain or trauma? When you delve into their pasts, do you see the patterns they inherited from their own parents? Doing so doesn't justify their actions but reveals that many are unaware of the cycles they're perpetuating. Reflect on your own moments of anger. Your reactions—aren't they sometimes echoes of a parent's behavior? These tendencies slip into our subconscious and can emerge even when we're determined not to replicate the hurt we've experienced.

Consider that your parents or guardians may have had similar reactions rooted in what they learned from their own upbringing. They, too, might have wished to act differently but were caught in patterns they didn't fully understand or know how to change. Their behaviors, often automatic and engaged in without self-awareness, may have been a constant, unwelcome presence in their lives. Your parents may have been doing the best they could with what they knew.

How can we find it within ourselves to forgive our parents, especially if they haven't offered a genuine apology? The path to forgiveness is through understanding the reasons behind their actions. As we unravel these reasons, we begin to take their behaviors less personally. We find empathy for what they didn't know and for resources they lacked. This, in turn, fosters our own growth, and gives us the opportunity to lead by example. They may never change. But through transforming our own life, we can show them what understanding, healing, and self-awareness make possible.

The hurtful actions of others—whether abuse, neglect, or other trauma-inducing behavior—stem from pain within themselves. These actions are reflections of their own internal struggles, which have created an imbalance within their five layers of energy. Emotionally, they're carrying a heavy load and don't know how to channel it except through outbursts that cause harm to themselves and others. Their muscular strength, which could have been channeled into constructive action, gets misdirected into acts of abuse or the passive aggression of abandonment. Their organs and glands suffer, too. Their adrenals are overworked and secreting stress hormones at unhealthy levels.

This could also be compounded by health issues. Many of those who have brought trauma into my life struggled with problems like hypertension, liver conditions, and gastrointestinal disorders. And as for their nervous system, it's always on high alert. I can't recall anyone who's hurt me who wasn't also deeply enmeshed in their own fight, flight, or freeze response.

Those who have inflicted trauma on us are often disconnected from their own minds, bodies, and emotions. Regardless of efforts others make to help them recognize their actions, many are entrenched in a victim mentality. They avoid taking personal responsibility for their lives and actions. Without a clear purpose or the tools to change their thoughts, physical habits, and emotional responses, they find themselves stuck in a repetitive cycle that operates beneath their awareness.

I forgave those like my mother who caused me pain because I came to understand their reasons. This isn't to say their actions were justified. But dwelling on those actions, demanding apologies, or clinging to resentment would only inhibit my personal growth.

EMBRACING YOUR ROLE

There will be days when you're too tired to pursue your health goals, feel embarrassed to show up as your authentic self, or don't want to forgive others' hurtful actions. In these moments, remind yourself who you are: a One Percenter.

Setbacks and difficulties are part of the journey. Embracing your role as a One Percenter means pushing through those tough times and to inspire those around you. Yes, it's challenging, especially with a sensitive nervous system, but you've overcome hardships before and achieved goals despite the odds. To do this, you need to consistently take responsibility for your actions, choices, and emotions, both in good and bad times. This doesn't mean beating yourself up over mistakes; it means applying the lessons and strategies you've learned and prioritizing your healing journey, even when faced with challenges. This lays the foundation for achieving emotional security.

Emotional security is stability and confidence in your emotional well-being. It means not being easily disturbed or thrown off balance by external events or internal feelings. This is the opposite of the emotional *in*security many of us have experienced all our lives as One Percenters. We've spent years living in survival mode, unable to truly meet our mental, physical, and emotional needs.

Whenever new stress enters your life—whether it's starting a new job, moving to a different environment, or dealing with a sick relative—your healing practices might fall by the wayside. We all have moments in which we are emotionally insecure. In those moments, we need to remind ourselves that overreacting to stress and losing focus on grounding ourselves back into our healing practices makes stress worse. Taking responsibility for your actions and making the best decisions for your emotional state as the world changes around you is what will help you continue to live your life as your most authentic self—the You You Never Knew—no matter what.

11

FEEL, LISTEN, AND ADJUST

Throughout this book, you have learned how trauma has imprinted on your nervous system and sensitized it. As you implement the healing protocols to manage your nervous system, you will start noticing differences. You will feel more at ease, your digestion will improve, your muscles will not be perpetually tight, and, in due time, you will be able to enter environments that used to overwhelm you without reacting as strongly as you did before. But there's one hard truth 1 must share with you: you are never truly "done" with healing from trauma.

Healing is an ongoing process that requires feeling the sensations of your sensitive nervous system, listening to what it tells you within the five layers of energy, and making the necessary adjustments. It requires constant awareness and the willingness to adapt to new challenges and changes.

You will experience times of significant growth, when you will feel a sense of accomplishment and progress. You will experience moments of peace and clarity that once seemed out of reach. These are the times to celebrate your resilience and the hard work you've put into your healing journey.

However, there will also be setbacks. There will be moments that test the progress you've made, when old triggers resurface and new ones emerge. These moments can be discouraging, but they are an essential part of the healing process. Setbacks do not erase the progress you've made; instead, they offer opportunities to deepen your understanding and reinforce your healing protocols. In fact, during the process of writing these last few chapters, I faced a challenge that put my own healing to the test.

It had been a rough month. I was tired, overworked, and feeling depleted when I received a phone call from the hospital. My mother had been assaulted, suffered brain damage, and was in a coma. I rushed to the hospital to see my mother lying unconscious in a hospital bed. I felt incapacitated, seconds away from breaking down. I wanted to cry as I stood over her, looking at the bruises and the deep cut that went from the top of her eyebrow to the back of her head.

I asked the detectives at the hospital what had happened. They couldn't identify who was responsible; they only knew it was a man who had assaulted her. My sorrow quickly turned into overwhelming anger and a desire for revenge. Then I remembered that my youngest brother, Daren, was by my side. He, too, had rushed to the hospital as soon as he received the news and, like me, was distraught and lost for words. Despite my exhaustion, sorrow, and anger, I was reminded of my Pursuit of Purpose, my *why*: to change my family's paradigm.

I walked over to Daren and said, "Hey, go home. I am going to take care of this. I will call you with updates."

Daren showed a sign of relief and said, "Are you sure? I know you have a lot of work to catch up with."

"Don't worry about that, bro. Go home and get some rest," I reassured him.

For the next few weeks, I sat in the hospital by my mother's side, fighting off negative thoughts by flipping the coin and maintaining a positive mental attitude during this challenging time. I would go home from the hospital to rest each night and return early the next morning. One morning, as I was driving back to the hospital, the nurse called me to tell me that my mother had come out of her coma. I was overwhelmed with joy and relief, feeling an immense wave of gratitude wash over me. Yet, I knew this was just the beginning of a long journey to full recovery.

During this time, I didn't miss a single day of work. My clients and online community repeatedly asked me the same question: "How were you able to manage yourself during this hard time without being overwhelmed by the stress and falling back on old habits?" My answer was simple: "By keeping my healing compass by my side."

THE HEALING COMPASS

Throughout my own journey and in my work with clients, I have relied on a powerful tool called the healing compass. This tool is a practical application of the healing protocols you have learned in this book. When you *feel* your nervous system getting out of balance due to stress, the healing compass helps you *listen* to the signs your body is giving you and make the necessary adjustments. It provides a clear and immediate way to realign yourself. The healing compass has kept me and my clients grounded and focused on our healing even during the most difficult moments.

The healing compass integrates the four main building blocks necessary to rewire the mind, body, and emotions: nutrition (N), Pursuit of Purpose (P), exercise (E), and rest (R). Each corresponds to a quadrant of the compass, which aligns these domains with specific layers of energy. By assessing each building block on a scale from 0 to 10, you can tally your overall energy score and reveal areas where you're experiencing imbalances or could be more consistent. This provides insight into areas for improvement and healing.

As outlined in Chapter 4, *nutrition* is essential for breaking the Trifecta Effect and managing a sensitive nervous system. It helps rewire energy layers involving the nervous system, organs, and glands. *Pursuit of Purpose*, as detailed in Chapter 6, is the motivator that sustains you—the core *why* that keeps you committed to your healing blueprint. Purpose is crucial for overcoming trauma and chronic stress. It rewires the energy layers connected to the subconscious mind and emotions. *Exercise*, which is discussed in Chapter 9 and includes strength training and the corrective exercises to fix an anterior pelvic tilt, is vital for rewiring the muscular system and triggering emotional release. Finally, *rest*, which is emphasized in Chapter 5, is essential for healing. Rest involves both sleep and relaxation activities that allow your body and mind to recover and rejuvenate. By promoting relaxation and reducing stress, rest allows

Nutrition
· Protein
· Low glycemic carbs
· Healthy fats

Pursuit of Purpose
· Integrating imagination
· Coin Flip Method
· Protecting your energy

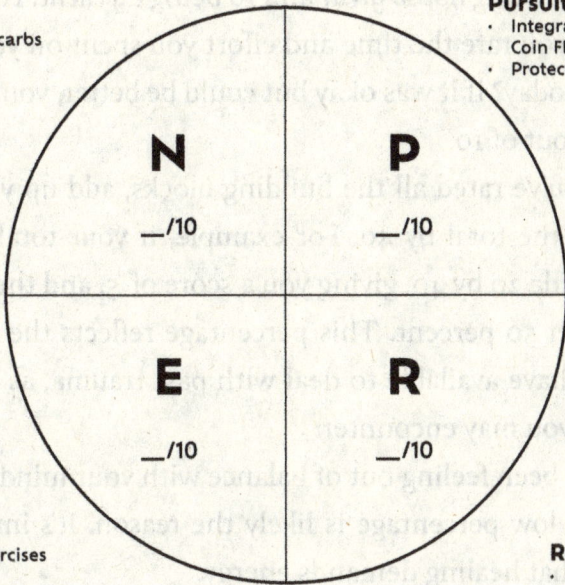

N __/10

P __/10

E __/10

R __/10

Exercise
· Corrective exercises
· Calisthenics
· Weight training

Rest
· Sleep
· I-we-all principle

Finding Your Final Score

Your Energy Scorecard
Score each area from 0 to 10 and add the scores together:
__/40
Energy Level (%) = (Total Score / 40) × 100
Your Energy Level: __%

each layer of energy to recover, regenerate, and function optimally, thus supporting holistic healing.

Taken together and performed with consistency, these building blocks rewire all five layers of energy and subconsciously shape the new you.

To use the healing compass, start by assessing your current habits within each of the four building blocks. As you can see, there is a blank space (__/10) next to each building block for you to fill in. I want you to rate yourself for each building block on a scale of

1 to 10, with 1 being *not so great* and 10 being *excellent*. For instance, how would you rate the time and effort you spent on your Pursuit of Purpose today? If it was okay but could be better, you might give yourself a 5 out of 10.

Once you've rated all the building blocks, add up your scores, then divide the total by 40. For example, if your total score was 20, then divide 20 by 40, giving you a score of .5, and then multiply by 100 to get 50 percent. This percentage reflects the amount of energy you have available to deal with past trauma, as well as the daily stress you may encounter.

If you've been feeling out of balance with your mind, body, and emotions, a low percentage is likely the reason. It's important to remember that healing demands energy.

Consider this analogy: imagine you had a long day of work ahead that relied heavily on your phone, but you had only charged your phone to 50 percent. When it eventually dies, you wouldn't immediately jump to the conclusion that there's something wrong with the phone. You wouldn't say your phone is "broken." Instead, you'd recognize that it simply hadn't had enough charge to last through the day.

Just as your phone isn't inherently flawed for running out of battery, you aren't "broken" if you are unable to cope with the impacts of past trauma or new stressors you encounter. The energy just isn't there. So, instead of focusing on the idea that you're broken, let's focus on how to effectively recharge. To heal stress and trauma, we need to make sure you're balanced and have the energy to do so.

Consider the building block with the lowest score as the starting point for your journey toward achieving better balance. It's often the area you neglect the most that needs your attention first. This doesn't mean you need to take drastic actions or make monumental changes right off the bat. Around each building block, there are reminders of actionable steps to gradually improve your balance and increase your score. Begin with small, manageable actions in these areas to strengthen the building block.

For example, if you scored lowest on your rest building block, your actions might be as simple as setting a regular bedtime. Even small changes can have a big impact when they're done consistently.

Don't feel overwhelmed if your scores aren't where you want them to be. Healing and growing are processes that take time. As you work on each building block, you'll naturally see improvements in other blocks and other areas of your life.

You may find it easier to improve certain blocks over others, but it's best to try balancing all the blocks. Focus on the block with the lowest score, working to improve it each day until its score matches your higher scores. Then move on to the next lowest score, and repeat this process. This way, you'll gradually bring all areas into balance. Remember, you're aiming for progress, not perfection. The longer you commit to and apply the information you've learned in this book, the more improvement you should see in your scores.

Our bodies are incredibly skillful at communicating with us, if only we take the time to listen. The way they signal us is through discomfort or pain. Pain is our body's SOS, an urgent call to address something that isn't working properly.

Reflect on a day when you're not getting adequate rest. How does your body respond? You'll likely experience fatigue, a persistent feeling of exhaustion that you can't shake off with a cup of coffee. What about when you've neglected exercise? You might have a nagging backache, a stiff neck, or an overall sense of lethargy. When applying your Pursuit of Purpose isn't part of your day, you may feel a heavy emotional weight, an internal pain that can be just as debilitating as any physical ailment. If your nutrition doesn't support your sensitive nervous system, it creates a domino effect of problems like digestive issues, anxiety, and muscular pain. The body is not our enemy, but our ally. Pain, in this context, becomes a language of the body that we must learn to understand and respect. By paying attention to pain signals and using the healing compass, we can address the underlying imbalances and begin our journey toward healing trauma and chronic stress.

When you feel out of balance, the healing compass will point you back toward equilibrium. You can revisit it as often as you need—daily or weekly. It keeps you on track and guides you to identify which building blocks require your attention, so that you're able to maintain the energy needed for healing.

When I first received the call about my mother's trauma, I felt overwhelmed with emotions, as if someone had pulled the ground out from under me. The healing compass helped me process these intense emotions without letting them consume me. I spent the first two nights at the hospital by her side and struggled with negative thoughts and emotions. I became impatient with the doctors for not having a solution to my mother's injuries as quickly as I would have liked. I realized my reactions were out of character and knew I needed to feel, listen, and adjust to navigate this traumatic experience without being consumed by my emotions.

My healing compass revealed that sleep was my lowest score. I had only slept two or three hours in the hospital, waking at every noise from the machines and whenever a nurse or doctor entered the room. I also noticed I wasn't eating properly. I was relying on snacks from the vending machines, triggering the Trifecta Effect.

As much as I wanted to go home to rest and improve my nutrition, I felt guilty about leaving my mother's side. However, I knew being tired and overwhelmed wouldn't be helpful to her. I applied the I-We-All principle—"I before We, and We before All"—from Chapter 5: if I take care of myself first by getting rest and breaking the Trifecta Effect, I can better support my mother during this difficult time. By consulting the healing compass, I was able to maintain my mind and body, ensuring I could be there for my mother when she needed me most.

ADJUSTING TO LIFE'S CHALLENGES

Feeling, listening, and adjusting isn't just about the four areas of the healing compass. It's necessary for all aspects of your personal development. Life never stays the same. Your purpose, environments, and even your dream team will evolve throughout your healing journey. Life's unpredictable nature can easily throw your nervous system off balance. Decisions must frequently be revisited and adjusted, even shortly after they're made. Adjustments are essential for personal growth and healing.

My own journey has seen significant shifts, from aspiring to be a basketball player to becoming a personal trainer and, now, a holistic health coach, content creator, and author. Along with these changes, my support network and environment have also shifted. As I pursued new goals, it became necessary to seek out new connections and build new support networks that aligned with my growth.

One of the biggest mistakes you can make during your healing journey is holding on to a previous purpose, environment, or dream team member when it's clear that it's time to move on. Trust your feelings. Listen to them. If it feels like it is time to adjust, do it. When fear arises, remind yourself that it's a sign of resistance, which may be a sign of your next call to adventure. Your next call emerges after you've accomplished some of your initial goals and signifies a new phase in your journey. Every new phase presents fresh challenges that require new adjustments.

Remember to flip the coin to reframe these challenges. If you feel anxious about distancing yourself from a friend who no longer supports your healing journey, see it as an opportunity to seek out more nurturing and understanding relationships for your dream team. Or, if you fear leaving a familiar but unhealthy environment, understand that this could be the first step toward creating a space that truly supports your well-being. When you embrace these moments with courage, you answer the next call to create a more fulfilling life.

Every adjustment I've ever made has turned out for the better, even when it didn't feel that way at first. As you transform into the new you, and as your goals transform, some or perhaps all of your dream team may not change with you. The environments that supported you at the beginning of your healing journey might not be supportive anymore. By adjusting, you're not losing something; those things are already lost. You are recognizing what isn't working and making the necessary changes in response. You can't make something work if it's inherently broken. You can only adapt and find new paths forward.

HEAL THE HEART, HEAL THE WORLD: OUR JOURNEY TO UNITY

One Sunday recently, my family gathered at my home for dinner. I cherish providing a safe place where loved ones can enjoy a meal, play board games, and engage in lively conversations, and I often find myself with my father in these moments, absorbing his wisdom. He remarked, "Pa, the world has changed so much since my days. I've never seen such disagreements, wars, and community division."

Reflecting on his words, I recognized this truth in my own life. I witnessed families split during the COVID-19 pandemic, communities divided during elections, and heightened awareness of global conflicts over race and religion.

During these challenging times, clients often ask me, "Nate, what do I do to manage my sensitive nervous system and stay calm and positive?" It's one of the most difficult questions I face as a coach and mentor. Throughout my life, I've trained my subconscious mind to stay positive, loving, and forgiving, even in the face of family divisions and street conflicts with friends. Yet, consciously, I've struggled to offer an answer that resonates with everyone, given their diverse beliefs.

Seeing even my father, a wise man known for his insights and answers, at a loss about the increasing challenges in the world reminded me of my own challenges when offering clear guidance to my clients. I abruptly stood up mid-conversation and grabbed my journal. I knew I needed to dig deeper into this issue. I believed that finding the root cause would help not only my father and me, but also my clients, and you.

Here is my answer, directly from my heart: we must understand that true solutions don't lie in external fixes but within each one of us. With constant media access, we are exposed to global conflicts, debates, environmental crises, political tensions, social injustices, public health concerns, economic fluctuations, and cultural clashes. This continuous influx of information keeps us informed, but it also frequently heightens our sense of distress, urgency, and personal struggles. The pain of division doesn't appear just in the world and in media; it's also in our homes, communities, and hearts.

For those of us who suffer from trauma and chronic stress, our heightened sensitivity and emotional intelligence can cause us to experience global tensions more intensely and persistently. In an unhealed state, we are vulnerable to a constant state of hyperarousal, perpetually on edge and primed for immediate reaction to challenges we cannot do very much about—at least not immediately or directly. However, by flipping the coin, we can transform this same sensitivity into our greatest strength. As we heal, this sensitivity allows us to more effectively feel, listen, and adjust, which better equips us to handle the constant stream of global issues presented by the media. By managing our reactions to these challenges, we reduce our distress, allowing us in turn to positively contribute to the world around us. We initiate a ripple effect that begins with us and extends to our homes, communities, and the world.

As you reflect on your own journey, consider how you can cultivate healing and unity in your daily life. How can you manage your reactions to stress and trauma to create a positive impact? By healing your mind, body, and emotions, you connect with your authentic self—the You You Never Knew. Focus on your own growth and well-being to inspire and uplift those around you. Share your healing journey with others, offer support to those in need, and encourage them to find their own paths to balance. Actively practice empathy and understanding in your interactions and seek to create positive change within your community. Together, we can foster a more harmonious and connected world.

THE YOU YOU NEVER KNEW

This journey began with a simple yet profound statement: you are not broken. As you turned these pages, you've seen this truth vividly demonstrated through my own experiences and the triumphs of my clients. You've seen firsthand that you are more than equipped for the challenges and transformation ahead. Your persistence and deep-rooted desire to become the best version of yourself is fueled by a soul that knows its capacity for healing.

As you close this book, remember that the journey doesn't end here. You carry within you the power to continue shaping your story—to become the You You Never Knew but have always been destined to become. Embrace this journey with an open heart, for in doing so, you light the path not just for yourself, but for all those you encounter along the way.

ACKNOWLEDGMENTS

This book is dedicated to my father, Nathan Turner. I would not be the man I am today without a father like you. Thank you for showing me the power of the mind and the laws of the universe. You never enforced a belief system on me; instead, you allowed me to be curious and educated me on anything I asked. You never gave up on me with my learning disabilities; it sometimes feels like you knew I would be in the position I am in today and wanted to ensure I was ready for it. During our worst times, you had incredible faith that everything would be okay, even when I didn't. You molded me to be fearless, which led me to believe I could go to the best basketball high school in the country, become the first Division I football player in school history, run a company at twenty-four, start my own business at twenty-six, make videos that have millions of views, and now write this book. Yes, your first son, who the doctors told you would never be able to live without assistance, who couldn't read or write, and who clung to your leg in the middle of the Holland Gardens projects surrounded by drug dealers and poverty, is now an author.

To my mother, Marybeth Hartwig, and my first client: I studied you, wanting to understand *why* you were the way you were. I sensed that your soul was young, lost, but joyful. From a very young age, I knew there was something deeper to the issues you had, and I felt it was the trauma your body had experienced. This is why I always forgave you, even after the trauma you inflicted on me. I knew that, deep down, your soul was working with a body that was disconnected. I studied you on meds, off meds, on drugs, during withdrawals, getting to know all sides of you as I learned to understand your bipolar disorder. I learned who you were by your body posture, the sound of your voice, the look in your eyes, and the noise you made in the house. This helped me adjust myself depending on which mom I was dealing with.

Since I was a little boy, I wanted to save you. I wanted to understand why you had your issues and empathized because I myself had some of your problems. I dedicate this book to you because no matter what I told you I wished to accomplish in my life, you never doubted me; you were one of my biggest cheerleaders. That alone was enough for me to push through doubt. If you had done the opposite, it would have killed my hope for better days. Because of you, I became obsessed with science and psychology, wanting to make connections between the mind, body, and emotions to help those who struggled like us. I do so with videos and podcasts, but now I get to share with the world through a book. Check that out,

Mom; you carried and gave birth to a young man who is helping the world one day at a time. You created me, I am you, and you should be proud.

To my younger brother, Brandon: reflecting on our shared past, your arrival in my life was a profound transformation. Growing up in Jersey City, New Jersey, I often felt isolated and different, particularly as the first child in our family with a Black father. My early years were fraught with challenges, from being teased about my stuttering and vitiligo to feeling alienated within our own family. But your presence, Brandon, changed everything. You saw past the boy burdened by bed-wetting and the awkwardness of a unique birthmark. To you, I was your brother, deserving of love and belonging.

Your resilience in the face of a world that treated you differently for your darker skin was nothing short of inspiring. Your courage and outspokenness helped me discover my own strength and determination. Together, we faced the world as an unbreakable team, united in the face of adversity. Your spirit—fierce, vocal, and authentically you—instilled in me a bravery that I carry to this day. The stories in this book are as much yours as they are mine. They capture our journey, a testament to rising above trauma, poverty, and abuse. We made it, Brandon. The promises I made during our hardest times—that hard work, positivity, and focusing on the good would bring success—have come true. This book is a tribute to the incredible impact you've had on my life. You are more than my little brother; you are an integral part of who I am.

To Daren, my baby brother: when you came into our lives, everything changed. You were born during our mother's imprisonment, and it was Aunt Kellie who first took you in. But our father ensured we cherished our time together. Those Fridays at the mall, followed by movies and weekends at the hotel, are unforgettable. They weren't just outings; they were moments of joy and unity. You always knew more than we thought, despite our efforts to protect you from our trauma. At twelve, you chose to leave Aunt Kellie's comfort to join our uncertain world. This decision, driven by the bond of brotherhood, amazed me. You didn't want to leave us behind, choosing a life with us over safety.

I promised you, as I did to Brandon, that if we worked hard and stayed positive, we could achieve anything. I spun a tale to inspire you. I pledged that you would go to private high school on a scholarship, tying it to my success in football. What started as a hopeful dream became a reality. My achievements in football led to your scholarship at St. Anthony's, proving that our beliefs could shape our destiny.

This book is a testament to that journey. It's a story of belief, perseverance, and the strength of our brotherhood. I hope it continues to inspire you and Brandon to believe in the power of dreams.

In the journey of writing this book and throughout the chapters where his teachings have left an indelible mark, I am profoundly grateful to Paul Chek and the CHEK Institute. As a student of the CHEK Institute, I have been fortunate to immerse myself in a wealth of knowledge that has deeply influenced my approach to holistic health. Paul's teachings resonate through the entirety of this work, and while they are specifically highlighted throughout this book, their impact extends far beyond. I sincerely thank Paul Chek and the CHEK Institute for their mentorship, wisdom, and invaluable resources, which have been instrumental in the development of this book.

To my agent, Coleen O'Shea, who believed in me and saw my vision. To my editor, Leah Wilson, who was my first choice since our initial conversation. To BenBella Books, for taking a chance on a first-time writer. And to Jeanne, my writing coach, who has always believed in my ability to become an author, even when my own belief wavered due to my learning disabilities. I am profoundly grateful to you all. Thank you.

To everyone who has been a part of my journey, both those mentioned in this book and those who silently walked alongside me, I extend my deepest gratitude. Each of you has contributed to the story of my life in ways that words can hardly capture. To the community of Jersey City, New Jersey—thank you for the lessons in resilience and toughness. The streets of our city, with their unspoken codes and challenges, have instilled in me a strength and determination that have been indispensable. The city, with all its complexities and character, has been a relentless teacher, shaping me into the person I am today.

To those who shared in my struggles, celebrated my victories, and provided support through my defeats, your impact has been profound. This book is not just a reflection of my experiences but also a tribute to each of you—to your influence, your belief, and your unwavering support.

NOTES

1   Bessel A. van der Kolk, "The Body Keeps the Score: Memory and the Evolving Psychobiology of Posttraumatic Stress," *Harvard Review of Psychiatry* 1, no. 5 (1994): 253–65. doi: 10.3109/10673229409017088. PMID: 9384857.

2   Bernet Elzinga, Christian Schmahl, Eric Vermetten, et al., "Higher Cortisol Levels Following Exposure to Traumatic Reminders in Abuse-Related PTSD," *Neuropsychopharmacology* 28, no. 9 (2003): 1656–65. doi:10.1038/sj.npp.1300226.

3   Hyoun K. Kim, Stacey S. Tiberio, Deborah M. Capaldi, et al., "Intimate Partner Violence and Diurnal Cortisol Patterns in Couples," *Psychoneuroendocrinology* 51 (2015): 35–46. doi.org/10.1016/j.psyneuen.2014.09.013. PMID: 25286224; PMCID: PMC4268378.

4   Andrew C. Dukowicz, Brian E. Lacy, and Gary M. Levine, "Small Intestinal Bacterial Overgrowth: A Comprehensive Review," *Gastroenterology & Hepatology* 3, no. 2 (2007): 112–22. PMID: 21960820; PMCID: PMC3099351.

5   Carol A. Kumamoto, "Inflammation and Gastrointestinal Candida Colonization," *Current Opinion in Microbiology* 14, no. 4 (2011): 386–91. doi:10.1016/j. mib.2011.07.015.

6   Louise Basmaciyan, Fabienne Bon, Tracy Paradis, et al., "Candida Albicans Interactions with the Host: Crossing the Intestinal Epithelial Barrier," *Tissue Barriers* 7, no. 2 (2019): 1612661. doi: 10.1080/21688370.2019.1612661.

7   Paul Chek, lecture notes from Holistic Lifestyle Coach Level 2, The CHEK Institute, 2021.

8   Hironori Kitade, Guanliang Chen, Yinhua Ni, et al., "Nonalcoholic Fatty Liver Disease and Insulin Resistance: New Insights and Potential New Treatments," *Nutrients* 9, no. 4 (2017): 387. doi:10.3390/nu9040387.

9   Roswitha Siener, Ihsan Machaka, Birgit Alteheld, et al., "Effect of Fat-Soluble Vitamins A, D, E and K on Vitamin Status and Metabolic Profile in Patients with Fat Malabsorption with and without Urolithiasis," *Nutrients* 12, no. 10 (2020): 3110. doi: 10.3390/nu12103110.

10 Valentine Y. Njike, Teresa M. Smith, Omree Shuval, et al., "Snack Food, Satiety, and Weight," *Advances in Nutrition* 7, no. 5 (2016): 866–78. doi: 10.3945/an.115.009340.

11 S. H. Lee, L. V. Moore, S. Park, D. M. Harris, et al. "Adults Meeting Fruit and Vegetable Intake Recommendations—United States, 2019," *Morbidity and Mortality Weekly Report* 71, no. 1 (2022): 1–9. doi:10.15585/mmwr.mm7101a1.

12 James J. DiNicolantonio and James O'Keefe, "The Importance of Maintaining a Low Omega-6/Omega-3 Ratio for Reducing the Risk of Autoimmune Diseases, Asthma, and Allergies," *Missouri Medicine* 118, no. 5 (2021): 453–59. PMID: 34658440; PMCID: PMC8504498.

13 Eric G. Krause, Annette D. de Kloet, Jonathan N. Flak, et al., "Hydration State Controls Stress Responsiveness and Social Behavior," *Journal of Neuroscience* 31, no. 14 (2011): 5470–76. doi:10.1523/JNEUROSCI.6078-10.2011.

14 S. Bhaskar, D. Hemavathy, and S. Prasad, "Prevalence of Chronic Insomnia in Adult Patients and Its Correlation with Medical Comorbidities," *Journal of Family Medicine and Primary Care* 5, no. 4 (2016): 780–84. doi: 10.4103/2249-4863.201153. PMID: 28348990; PMCID: PMC5353813.

15 Paul Chek, lecture notes from Holistic Lifestyle Coach Level 2, The CHEK Institute, 2021.

16 Ibid.

17 Ibid.

18 Shwetha Nair, Mark Sagar, John Sollers III, et al., "Do Slumped and Upright Postures Affect Stress Responses? A Randomized Trial," *Health Psychology* 34, no. 6 (2015): 632–41. doi:10.1037/hea0000146.

INDEX

ABOUT THE AUTHOR

Overcoming a tough past of homelessness and struggles, **Nate Ortiz** turned his life around and is now a renowned celebrity life and health coach, and social media influencer. Known as the lifestyle coach for those ready for change, Nate uses his past experiences and reengineered mindset to help people create their dream life.

Growing up in a turbulent family with addiction and incarceration, Nate faced numerous hardships, but he learned the power of exercise and positive communication when his stepfather returned from jail transformed and inspired him to shift his life. Turning pain into power, Nate became a motivator and an influencer.

Today, with a Bachelor of Science in movement science and certifications in nutrition, personal training, holistic lifestyle, and integrative health coaching, he's made a name for himself. As a speaker, he captivates audiences from school groups to TV viewers with his inspiring journey. Influencing lives across various platforms, including YouTube, Instagram, and his podcast, Nate is a beacon of inspiration. By sharing his story and expertise, he not only lives his dream life but empowers others to reach their goals, too. Find him online at www.begreatwithnate.com.